E-COMMERCE SECURITY
AND PRIVACY

ADVANCES IN INFORMATION SECURITY

E-COMMERCE SECURITY AND PRIVACY

edited by

Anup K. Ghosh
Cigital, Inc., U.S.A.

KLUWER ACADEMIC PUBLISHERS
Boston / Dordrecht / London

Distributors for North, Central and South America:
Kluwer Academic Publishers
101 Philip Drive
Assinippi Park
Norwell, Massachusetts 02061 USA
Telephone (781) 871-6600
Fax (781) 871-6528
E-Mail < kluwer@wkap.com >

Distributors for all other countries:
Kluwer Academic Publishers Group
Distribution Centre
Post Office Box 322
3300 AH Dordrecht, THE NETHERLANDS
Telephone 31 78 6392 392
Fax 31 78 6546 474
E-Mail < services@wkap.nl >

 Electronic Services < http://www.wkap.nl >

Library of Congress Cataloging-in-Publication Data

E-commerce security and privacy / edited by Anup K. Ghosh.
    p. cm. — (Advances in information security ; 2)
   Includes bibliographical references and index.
   ISBN 0-7923-7399-5 (alk. paper)
   1. Computer security. 2. Privacy, Right. 3. E-commerce—Security measures. I. Ghosh,
Anup K. II. Series.

   QA76.9.A25 R433 2001
   005.8—dc2

                                    2001034439

Printed on acid-free paper.

Printed in the United States of America

The Publisher offers discounts on this book for course use and bulk purchases.
For further information, send email to < susan.lagerstrom-fife@wkap.com >

Contents

List of Figures

List of Tables

Contributing Authors

Annie I. Antón is the Asea Brown Boveri Assistant Professor of Software Engineering in the North Carolina State University College of Engineering. She is Co-Director of the NC State E-Commerce Studio, recipient of an NSF CAREER Award, and a member of the IEEE and the ACM.

Brad Arkin is a founding member of the Software Security Group at Cigital, Inc. He helps Cigital's clients build and operate security critical software.

Mikhail J. Atallah is a professor in the Computer Sciences Department at Purdue University. Dr. Atallah received a BE degree in electrical engineering from the American University, Beirut, Lebanon, in 1975, and MS and Ph.D. degrees in electrical engineering and computer science from Johns Hopkins University, Baltimore, Maryland, in 1980 and 1982, respectively.

Andre Dos Santos joined the Georgia Tech College of Computing faculty in the fall of 2000 as an Assistant Professor. His research interests are in all aspects of computer security, but focus particularly on the security and use of tamper resistant devices such as smart cards, the security of Internet technologies and applications, and the security of online banking systems and online brokerage.

Wenliang Du is currently a Ph.D. student in the Department of Computer Sciences and the Center for Education and Research in Information Assurance and Security (CERIAS) at Purdue University.

Julia B. Earp is an Assistant Professor in the North Carolina State University College of Management. She is Co-Director of the NC State

E-Commerce Studio, Director of the NCSU Internet Security and Privacy Project and is a member of the IEEE and ACM.

Anup K. Ghosh is Director of Security Research at Cigital, Inc. He is author of *Security and Privacy for E-Business* (Wiley, 2001) and *E-Commerce Security: Weak Links, Best Defenses* (Wiley, 1998).

Marc Goodman is the Chief Cybercriminologist for the information security consultancy AtomicTangerine. Mr. Goodman is a member of Interpol's global steering committee on information technology crime and is the former Officer-in-Charge of the Los Angeles Police Department's Internet Unit.

Sushil Jajodia is BDM Professor and Chairman of the Department of Information and Software Engineering and Director of Center for Secure Information Systems at the George Mason University, Fairfax, Virginia. His email address is jajodiagmu.edu and the his web page address is http://isse.gmu.edu/ csis/faculty/jajodia.html.

Richard A. Kemmerer is a Professor and past Chair of the Department of Computer Science at the University of California, Santa Barbara. His research interests include formal specification and verification of systems, computer system security and reliability, programming and specification language design, and software engineering.

Michiharu Kudo received the B.E. degree and M.E. degree from Tokyo University, Tokyo, Japan, in 1986 and 1988, respectively. He is currently a researcher at IBM Tokyo Research Laboratory.

V.S. Subrahmanian is Professor of Computer Science at the University of Maryland, College Park. He has worked extensively on heterogeneous data and software integration, software agents, multimedia databases, probabilistic and temporal databases, and computational logic systems.

Vijay Varadharajan is Microsoft Chair Professor of Computing at Macquarie University and is the Director of Information and Networked Systems Security Research. He is also the Technical Board Director of Australian Computer Society.

Giovanni Vigna is an Assistant Professor in the Department of Computer Science at the University of California in Santa Barbara. His current research interests include network and computer security, intrusion detection systems, security of mobile code systems, penetration testing, and distributed systems.

Hongxue Wang is an associate professor at Athabasca University, Canada. His areas of interest include intelligent system modeling, electronic commerce, computer security, and distance education.

Yan Zhang is a senior lecturer at University of Western Sydney, Australia. His research interests include logic and knowledge-based systems.

Foreword

Welcome to the second volume of the Kluwer International Series on ADVANCES IN INFORMATION SECURITY. The goals of this series are, one, to establish the state of the art of and set the course for future research in information security and, two, to serve as a central reference source for advanced and timely topics in information security research and development. The scope of this series includes all aspects of computer and network security and related areas such as fault tolerance and software assurance.

ADVANCES IN INFORMATION SECURITY aims to publish thorough and cohesive overviews of specific topics in information security, as well as works that are larger in scope or that contain more detailed background information than can be accommodated in shorter survey articles. The series also serves as a forum for topics that may not have reached a level of maturity to warrant a comprehensive textbook treatment.

The success of this series depends on contributions by researchers and developers such as yourself. If you have an idea for a book that is appropriate for this series, I encourage you to contact either the Acquisitions Editor for the series, Lance Wobus (lwobus@wkap.com), or myself, the Consulting Editor for the series (jajodia@gmu.edu). We would be happy to discuss any potential projects with you. Additional information about this series can be obtained from www.wkap.nl/series.htm/ADIS.

About this volume

The second volume of this series is entitled *Recent Advances in E-Commerce Security and Privacy*, edited by Anup K. Ghosh.

Electronic commerce represents a tremendous opportunity and difficult challenge for security researchers and practitioners. Business-to-consumer (B2C) and business-to-business (B2B) applications are rapidly changing the way we conduct business these days. However, how we can do this while protecting both businesses and consumers from theft and false representation continues to be an open problem. Solutions that are being deployed in the marketplace have often been ad hoc in nature, and there is a need to provide a principled theoretical foundation. This volume brings together contributions from a number of respected researchers to address this need.

It has been a pleasure working with the editor of this volume, Anup K. Ghosh, who is a world-renowned expert in electronic commerce security. He is a noted speaker and the author of *Security and Privacy for E-Business* (Wiley, 2001) and *E-Commerce Security: Weak Links, Best Defenses* (Wiley, 1998).

SUSHIL JAJODIA
Consulting Editor

Preface

The Internet has fundamentally changed much of the way most of us do business now. Electronic commerce (or e-commerce) in its many myriad forms utilizes technology to connect people and facilitate business. Business-to-business e-commerce transactions are expected to exceed US $6 trillion by 2006. Perhaps more revealing of how e-commerce is changing the commercial landscape is that e-commerce transactions are expected to account for 25% of all retail transactions in the next decade.

Throughout the period of meteoric growth in e-commerce, the security risks have grown similarly in scope and magnitude. Three major factors have driven the security risks in e-commerce: first, the sole reliance on the electronic medium for a company's core business, second, the growing complexity of the software systems needed to support e-commerce, and third, the value of the digital assets brought online to an inherently insecure medium — the Internet.

While security has long been a primary concern in e-commerce, more recently, *privacy* concerns have become the number one concern for consumers. Many of the same Internet technologies that make e-commerce possible, also make it possible to create detailed profiles of an individual's purchases, to spy on individual Web usage habits, and even to peer into confidential files that reside on the individual's machine.

While much has been written in the popular literature about electronic commerce risks, this volume is the first to pull together leading researchers and practitioners in different fields of computer science and software engineering to present their technical innovations to problems in security and privacy in e-commerce. This book draws from selected papers presented at the first Workshop on Security and Privacy in E-Commerce (WSPEC'00) held in Athens, Greece, November 4, 2000. The papers were selected for their quality and also for the breadth in topics in e-commerce security and privacy they represent.

The book is divided into two parts: (1) selected case studies in electronic commerce security, and (2) reasoning about secure and private electronic commerce. The first part is aimed at the practitioner who seeks understanding and insight into problems encountered in electronic commerce security and privacy as well as practical solutions.

In the first part of the book, we present two case studies on analyzing the security of e-commerce systems. The first case study assumes no first hand knowledge of the software that runs an online banking system, while the second provides a case study into working with an organization and its software to identify and mitigate problems in an online gambling operation. The third case study examines new problems that arise in mobile e-commerce — an emerging field that is taking advantage of wireless Internet connectivity to handheld devices. The final case study examines the technical and legal problems facing law enforcement in identifying and prosecuting transnational computer crimes. The case study shows that while the Internet knows no geographic boundaries, law enforcement is faced with considerable jurisdictional hurdles in tracking and prosecuting malicious hackers.

The second part of this book is more formal and is aimed at the researcher interested in state-of-the-art innovations in reasoning about secure and private e-commerce. Many of the articles in this section provide a framework about which to reason how a given protocol or system of e-commerce meets security and privacy requirements.

The first article in the second part provides a goal-based approach for specifying security and policy requirements into operational system requirements. The second article in this part addresses a timely issue: how to ensure secure and private access to Internet databases. The authors provide several protocols for secure remote access to online databases aimed at providing secure and private transactions for very confidential queries, such as to medical databases. The third article in this part provides a logic system for reasoning about accountabilities in cryptographic protocols for e-commerce. The final article provides a logic system for provisional authorizations in e-commerce transactions. The authors demonstrate the utility of provisional authorization to two types of e-commerce systems: electronic auctions and business-to-business e-commerce transactions.

In summary, this book provides both practitioners and researchers with innovations in secure and private e-commerce. Practitioners will gain great insight from the case studies, and researchers will be able to learn about state-of-the-art protocols in secure and private e-commerce that will serve as the basis for future innovations in applied e-commerce technologies.

Since the book is a collection or articles, the reader can jump straight to the chapters of interest without losing context from earlier chapters.

Speaking on behalf of all contributing authors, we believe the innovations contained in this book will blaze the trail for a more secure and private system of e-commerce in the future.

ANUP K. GHOSH

Acknowledgments

This book is a compilation of articles from many contributors. The contributors deserve much credit and appreciation for their time and dedication to preparing these articles for publication.

There were many individuals who also helped pull together the first Workshop on Security and Privacy in E-Commerce in Athens, Greece, from which selected papers were chosen for this volume. Foremost among them, Dimitris Gritzalis from the Athens University of Economics & Business deserves much credit for hosting and pulling together the workshop. In addition, this workshop was in large part the brainchild of Sushil Jajodia of George Mason University. The arduous efforts of the program committee in reviewing and selecting papers presented in the workshop also deserve much credit: Yair Frankel, Dimitris Gritzalis, Sushil Jajodia, Nikos Kyrloglou, Gary McGraw, Fabian Monrose, Pierangela Samarati, Tomas Sander, Sang Son, Bhavani Thuraisingham, Win Treese, Vijay Varadharajan, and Giovanni Vigna.

Finally, those who support us both at home and at work probably deserve the most credit for making possible the contributions in this book. We thank you all for your continued support.

I

CASE STUDIES IN E-COMMERCE SECURITY

Chapter 1

SECURITY TESTING OF AN ONLINE BANKING SERVICE

Andre L.M. dos Santos
Reliable Software Group
Department of Computer Science
University of California, Santa Barbara
andre@cs.ucsb.edu

Giovanni Vigna
Reliable Software Group
Department of Computer Science
University of California, Santa Barbara
vigna@cs.ucsb.edu

Richard A. Kemmerer
Reliable Software Group
Department of Computer Science
University of California, Santa Barbara
kemm@cs.ucsb.edu

Abstract

Online banking and electronic commerce have become an everyday reality for millions of users. Almost every large banking institution offers services such as account management, fund transfers, automatic payments, and investments through the Internet. The quality of the provided services has become a driving factor in user selection of a banking institution. Given the critical nature of the services provided, banks and financial institutions are investing substantial resources in the implementation of sophisticated financial applications that are appealing to the end-user. In the design and implementation of these applications developers face a trade-off between user-friendliness and security.

This chapter presents the results of the security testing of the online banking services of a large international bank. The testing process followed a purely black-box approach. Starting from a single legitimate account and unprivileged Internet access to the bank's site it was possible to compromise the security of many accounts. The results of the study show how user-friendliness may clash with security requirements leading to critical flaws in the system. The lessons learned from this experiment represent an initial step towards a more careful design of online financial applications.

Introduction

Today, millions of users access financial services through the Internet [Ghosh, 1998]. Online banking offers many advantages to the banks, which reduce their operating costs and reach a larger portion of their clientele, and to the users, which receive 24 hours a day/7days a week banking services from their homes and workplaces.

The services offered range from simple account management to fund transfers and online investments. The volume of the online transactions performed may vary from a few dollars to thousands of dollars, but the overall volume of the transactions is large and is destined to become a substantial portion of the banking services. In this scenario, banks and financial institutions struggle to captivate users through the provision of sophisticated services and appealing, user-friendly applications.

These applications suffer from the problems of any Internet- and World Wide Web-based application. The large-scale distributed nature of the application architecture, the use of an insecure communication infrastructure, such as the Internet, the use of WWW technology, which historically suffers from many security flaws [Paoli et al., 1998, Dean et al., 1996], and the requirements of the users in terms of usability make the design of a secure online banking service a difficult task. In addition, the reduced time-to-market and the need to reach a wide range of users put tremendous pressure on the application developers, sometimes leading to insecure implementations. In the past, flaws in online banking applications have been exploited by hackers to compromise the security of user accounts. These attacks are seldom publicized because of the impact that they may have on users' confidence in the compromised financial institutions. Yet, it is important to evaluate how flaws may appear in these systems in an effort to develop a set of methodologies, techniques, and guidelines that may help the application developer to deliver secure and user-friendly online banking applications.

This chapter describes the security testing performed against the online banking services of Bank X, a large international bank with more than 30 million accounts and approximately 400,000 online accounts. Security testing (also known as "penetration testing") aims at determining weaknesses in the security protections of a system. There are very few documented experiments like the one described in this chapter. Banks are usually not happy to have their security flaws exposed. In addition, the testers often don't want to discuss their approaches and techniques.

The experiment is interesting also because it shows an example of the trade-offs between security and user-friendliness. As it will be explained later, the adoption of user-defined personal identification numbers (PINs) and meaningful error messages disclosed security-critical information during the attack. In addition, this case study shows how vulnerable these systems are to social engineering attacks.

The remainder of this chapter is structured as follows. Section 1 describes the approach that was followed in the testing process. Section 2 describes the architecture of the on-line system under attack. Section 3 details the actual testing process. Finally, Section 4 draws some conclusions and discusses the lessons learned from this experiment.

1.   The approach

The goal of this security testing process was to compromise one or more accounts using the online banking service. Compromise includes access to private information (e.g., access to the account balance) and the ability to transfer funds from the attacked account to another.

The approach followed is pure *black-box testing*. That is, no information other than the name of the web site providing the service was known prior to the beginning of the attacks. We acted as "hackers" interested in penetrating or circumventing the security protections of Bank X's network-based services. However, our approach differed from a real attack in two ways. First, we took extra precautions not to jeopardize the mission of Bank X. This of course would not be a concern if we were malicious hackers. For example, some attacks that may have disrupted the infrastructure were performed during a well-defined time window that was determined by interacting with the security officers of Bank X. Second, we did not use any caution in hiding our attempts to probe for and then exercise security vulnerabilities in the online banking system. This was done to test the ability of Bank X to detect and record even the most blatant attack signatures.

At the beginning of the study we had no idea what the protocols used by the applications were, what the account number format was, or even what the account lockout procedure was. Before starting the attacks we opened a legitimate account at one of Bank X's branches. The account was accessible online, and it helped us to determine what protocols and message formats were used.

The study was a several month effort that began in November 1998 and ended in January 1999. The study revealed weaknesses in the online system and identified vulnerable areas that resulted in a major redesign of the system. This document is the first authorized disclosure of the attack against Bank X.

2.   The online banking system

Bank X's online banking system is based on WWW technology. A user connects to a web server using a web browser. TCP/IP connections between the client and the server are protected against eavesdropping by means of the SSL protocol [Freier et al., 1996].

The user begins an online banking session by filling in four text fields of an applet or HTML form. These fields are: branch number, account number, control digit, and PIN. The sizes of these fields are:

- branch number: maximum of 4 digits;

- account number: maximum of 6 digits;

- control digit: 1 digit;

- PIN: 4 digits.

Bank X is very concerned about their online banking system being user-friendly. In order to achieve this goal, specific information is returned to the user in case one or more of the fields are filled with incorrect information. In addition, this is done in an ordered and deterministic way. That is, first the branch number is checked. If the check fails, the system will generate an answer saying that the branch number is incorrect. Then the application checks if the control digit is correct with respect to the account number. If it is not so, a message saying that the control digit is incorrect is returned. If the control digit is correct for the given account number, then the account is checked. The account may be non-existent or not registered for Internet access. In each case, a different answer is returned. Finally, the system generates a specific answer for an incorrect PIN.

The system has an additional authentication procedure. After filling the fields with correct information another web page is presented to the user. This page has one or two HTML form fields depending on whether it is a business account or a personal account. These fields are used to request personal information, such as SSN, EIN, or mother's maiden name. The system logs the user in only after checking the correctness of this information.

Thus, in order for a user to log into his/her account, he/she needs to give correct answers for the challenges of two different web pages. That is, the user needs to enter a correct branch number, account number, control digit and PIN in the first web page, and after this the user needs to fill the correct personal information, related to the specific account in a second web page. After the information has been validated by the server, the user is presented with a web page that gives the ability to check balance, perform transfers, change personal information, and pay bills.

3. The attack

The attack was carried out through a series of steps. In the following sections the steps are presented sequentially, but the actual testing sometimes required backtracking to previous steps.

3.1. Understanding the services

The first step of the attack was to leverage off of the legitimate account under our control to determine the characteristics of the service, such as its general structure and the lockout policy.

The online banking system locks out after entering either three wrong PINs or two wrong personal data items. The lock out happens even if the second wrong personal data is entered after the attacker enters one wrong personal data and exits the system; i.e., the system maintains status information across sessions. The experiments also determined that the lock outs are reset every day at midnight.

During this phase our efforts were concentrated on reverse engineering of the applet used on the client side. The bank's application was a Java applet that used three Java classes for account authentication. These classes had names that were random and unique for each page hit. This protected the application against an attack where a malicious user infiltrates a Trojan horse Java class in order to get control of a site's applet [dos Santos, 1997].

The bank applet's Java classes were obfuscated in order to make it harder for someone to disassemble or decompile them. As a result, the Javasoft JDK disassembler was not able to disassemble these classes, and the Mocha and Jasmine decompilers were not able to decompile them. In order to fix this we developed a pre-decompiler. This pre-decompiler cleans up the classes' bytecode by modifying two patterns that were discovered not to be properly formatted.

Both patterns were related to the number used for the size of the parameters inside the class file. According to the Java virtual machine specification [Lindholm and Yellin, 1999] many parameters in a Java class file have variable size and as such must have their size in bytes explicitly specified. The first obfuscation was accomplished by declaring strings in the "constant_pool" array of a class file to be of a bigger size than they really were. This was identified by the pre-compiler by searching for the null byte (00) at the end of the string. This byte belonged to the next declaration in the "constant_pool" and indicated the real end of the string. The other obfuscation was accomplished by inflating a line feed byte (0A) to be a line feed plus carriage return byte (0A 0D) without updating the size of the parameter. This meant that the parameter was declared with a smaller size than it really was. This was fixed by collapsing any combination of line feed plus carriage return into a line feed byte.

The three obfuscated classes used for account authentication were de-compiled by Jasmine after being processed by the pre-decompiler. These classes provided the functionality for a user interface, a crypto algorithm, and an interface to the crypto algorithm. The crypto algorithm was not studied to verify its correctness or security.

3.2.   Development of a custom application

The successful reverse engineering of the client side applet allowed us to develop a Java application that interacted directly with Bank X's site. The application used two of the three original classes with very little modification. The Bank X applet, and therefore our application, uses a timestamp that is supposed to control how long a request may live. The timestamp is obtained by performing a get operation to a specific URL. This information is provided for any request and can be acquired every time the application needs to encode information to be sent to the server. This solution was not attractive, however, due to the network delay between requests and replies. Instead, the local clock was synchronized with the bank clock at start time.

The four text fields (branch number, account number, control digit, and PIN) are encrypted together with the timestamp by the crypto class. An HTTP GET request is performed by the Java applet after converting the encrypted information to a string. The return value of the GET request is a nonce. The nonce is then used to perform a second GET request that returns a page, which is shown in the user's browser where the original applet is running. This page either requests personal information data or reports that some of the fields were filled incorrectly.

The applet uses the `showDocument` method to display this page. Our Java application, on the other hand, is only interested in parsing this page to get the values returned. Therefore, the application stops after receiving enough of the page contents to allow it to identify the answer received.

It should be noted that the nonce can be used only once (as it should be). This means that if an attacker hijacked or fabricated a nonce, then there is a chance that he could use it before the legitimate user does. This would allow the attacker to fetch the second page of the online banking system, which requests personal information. The nonce by itself does not give away information about the account number for which it was generated, but the page that is fetched using the nonce implicitly has this information. Thus, an attacker could possibly gain access to a user's account with a good database of personal information and a valid nonce. The attacker could also use the lock out procedure to deny service to the rightful user while and after performing an attack that hijacks a nonce.

3.3. Determining valid branch and account numbers

The experiments performed on the online system attempted to find out what accounts existed, whether they were Internet-accessible, what the PIN number for each account was, who owned the accounts, and eventually gain complete access to the accounts on the online system. A series of experiments were performed to see how difficult it would be to get any or all of this information. These experiments were performed by using Bank X's online banking services at Bank X's site, as well as by social engineering. The following subsections describe the experiments and their success.

The first experiment that was run attempted to demonstrate that the valid accounts for a particular branch could be readily determined, but this required first determining the valid branch numbers. Finding branch numbers is relatively easy, since branch numbers for all Bank X branches are available at Bank X's web site. Thus, an attacker can select the branches that are most interesting (e.g., those in large cities) and attack them.

As already mentioned, account numbers are composed of a six digit number and an additional control digit. When we first started this experiment we tried all ten possible control digits for each account number tried. Using this approach it was necessary to test an average of five control digits before finding the correct one. For each attempt an answer saying "bad control digit" indicated that a wrong control digit was tried. After collecting more than 300 correct account numbers and corresponding control digits we were able to correctly reverse engineer the algorithm that is used to generate the control digit.

We do not know if the algorithm used for the generation of this control digit is in the public domain, but because it was not available to us we were forced to determine it by reverse engineering. By using the control digit generation algorithm, answers saying that the control digit or branch number are incorrect were eliminated. The remaining answers enabled us to map a branch with regard to accounts that were in use and those that were accessible through the Internet. As a bonus, if an account used the PIN that was tried, this was reported too.

3.4.   Determining valid PINs

Many online banking services rely on a fixed length personal identification number (PIN) to identify a user. Some banks, allow access to all of their online operations after a successful PIN is entered; others require additional identification, like social security number, mother's maiden name or an additional PIN.

As with passwords, users have difficulty in remembering large personal identification numbers. Therefore, there is a natural tendency to use small, easy to remember numbers (like birthday or 1234). Anticipating the problems that this class of numbers can represent, many Internet banking applications require users to choose PINs that are not easy to guess. In the interest of user-friendliness, however, the banks cannot require the user to use, and remember, a very large number. Therefore, it is a wide spread practice to use 4 or 6 digit PINs. Unfortunately, because of the small size of the PINs, an attacker can target a particular account and try all possibilities. In order to defend against this class of attacks, banks usually lock out accounts after a certain number of unsuccessful identification attempts.

The success of our attack relied on the ratio between the size of the personal identification number and the number of users of the service. If we were to fix the account and vary the possible PINs this would cause a lock out in the particular account after a minimal number of failures. Instead, we fixed the PIN and varied the account number. This resulted in no lock outs, since a particular account will be tried again with a different PIN only after numerous other accounts have been tried. Thus, the lock out protection is not triggered. Some banks, however, rely on an additional IP-triggered protection that locks out specific IP addresses after a certain number of failed attempts from the same IP address. This can be bypassed by means of IP spoofing [Bellovin, 1990]. Bank X used this additional lock out mechanism.

Because the bank PIN numbers are only four digits long, there are only 10,000 possible PIN values. This small number of PIN values coupled with the large number of online accounts (390,000) makes a random PIN guessing attack very attractive to the attacker. If the PIN numbers were uniformly distributed and the PIN number guess was randomly generated, then the guess would be successful in matching the correct PIN for one in every 10,000 accounts tried (i.e., .01%). Thus, 39 accounts would have their PIN compromised for every PIN number guessed. Unfortunately, the common use of easy to guess PINs makes the system even more vulnerable. When we ran the first experiment, which mapped accounts for each branch, we used the PIN 1234. This experiment revealed that 3% of the online users from the test branches were using PIN 1234.

When running the account mapping experiment it was discovered that the transaction speed using the Internet at the test site varied significantly. This could be viewed as an advantage for the bank in discouraging attackers. We found, however, that even with this variation the average time required to test one account was only six seconds. Using this average and noting that account numbers can go up to 999999, it would take 6,000,000 seconds or about 70 days to test all possible accounts at a single branch. This time could be reduced significantly, however, by performing parallel accesses. When running the experiments we determined that the delay was mostly caused by the reduced bandwidth and not by server saturation. To verify this, three applications were run in parallel and it was observed that the throughput for each application had not changed significantly from the throughput observed when only one application was running.

Another observation that was made when mapping the valid accounts was that the branches give preference to low numbered accounts. As a result, an attacker could successfully map a large portion of the valid accounts by starting with account 1 and trying account numbers in order up to a prefixed value. We found that trying values lower than 100,000 gave good results in the experiments.

3.5.   Finding account owners

After determining the valid accounts with online banking access and their associated PINs, the next step was to determine the name of the account owner. This is important information for the attacker, and it is sensitive information to the bank. One might think that it would be difficult for the attacker to find out this information. Our experimentation showed that with access to one legitimate account it is trivial to get all account owners of valid accounts in a branch, with very few exceptions.

To find account owners an attacker with access to an account only needs to use the transfer facility of the online banking system. To be more specific, the attacker initiates a transfer from his/her account to the account for which he/she wants to know the owner. This action causes the server to return a page that contains the name of the owner of the account and that asks for confirmation of the transfer. Now that the attacker has the desired information, he/she can record it and cancel the transfer operation. In a few cases this approach wasn't successful because the account was either "blocked" or "non-authorized".

To demonstrate the feasibility of this approach for identifying the owner of an account a program was developed that repetitively performed the operation of initiating a transfer and aborting it. The program generated transfer requests using a valid login to the system using the account to which we had legitimate access. One inconvenience that had to be overcome was that a session in the online banking system has a fixed lifetime. That is, the session is no longer valid after some time. To overcome this the program recognizes when the lifetime expires, and, when necessary, it logs into the system again starting a new session.

3.6.   Finding personal information

The final step to achieve complete access to the accounts is to answer one or more questions about the owner of the account. More specifically, the applet embedded in the first page of the online banking system, which is emulated by the developed application, returns a nonce. This nonce is then used to construct a URL that is used to fetch an HTML page. In the case where the correct PIN number was entered, this page requests information based on the account owner's personal data. On this page it is explicitly stated that the personal data is randomly selected. When running the experiments we found that for personal accounts the system requested two different pieces of data each time, and these were requested in a non-deterministic way. The two requests were chosen from SSN, date of birth, father's name, and mother's maiden name. For company accounts the information requested was always the company's tax identification number, EIN.

To obtain information about personal account holders we first decided to use social engineering. We assumed that we would have a better chance of obtaining the required information for a branch in a small town where we had access to people who might know personal information about the individual that owned the account. Thus, to test our assumption we focused on a branch from a small town and repeated the experiments presented above. In a matter of a few hours we were able to obtain the PINs for 25 accounts at that branch. Using the name of the owner of one of these accounts we were able to obtain the required personal information by asking questions of someone in the town. This enabled us to completely compromise our first account.

We were not completely satisfied with the approach since it required the attacker to obtain the personal data by social engineering, which could be very time consuming. In addition, this type of social engineering adds more risk for a potential attacker. Therefore, we decided to investigate how difficult it could be to get the personal information that is needed from publicly available data sources outside the bank system. We found that we were able to call the governmental department in charge of distributing SSNs and EINs, and get these numbers. To demonstrate the feasibility of this approach, we used this method to compromise two personal accounts and two business accounts. One of the business accounts was for a well-known foreign corporation.

In analyzing how personal information is requested by the online system and how the answers are returned, we discovered some critical weaknesses in the approach. In particular, we discovered that we were able to choose which personal information to return to the system, regardless of what information was requested. To be more specific, the server does not keep track of what questions were asked. Instead, it uses the text field name in the page to determine what was requested. Therefore, by changing the text field appropriately, we were able to answer the questions that we knew the answer to, rather than the questions that we were asked[1]. Thus, an account could be compromised even if only some of the information that could be requested was known. A more thorough analysis of this part of the system revealed that for business accounts the personal information requests could be completely bypassed. Recall that for business accounts the EIN was always requested. It is not difficult to find out the EIN of a company, but we found an even easier approach. When asked for an EIN we again changed the field name in our coded response. However, instead of giving the answer to the question asked we gave an answer stating that the name of the father is "null". Since business accounts never have a father, the system validated this answer and logged us into the company's account. This turned out to be particularly useful because we had previously found that for some special accounts we were unable to get the name of the business or person that owned the account. Our routine identified these accounts as "non-authorized". For these accounts it was impossible to get the necessary personal data using the publicly available data sources outside the bank. However, with the bypass method, this was no longer necessary. To demonstrate the feasibility of this approach, we used the bypass method to compromise the account of a large multinational corporation, which regularly performed transfers of $100,000 or more.

4. Conclusions

The security testing performed against Bank X's online banking system was successful in compromising a number of accounts. We developed an approach to collect valid account numbers and PINs and a second approach to automatically associate these accounts with the person or business that owned the account. This information could then be used to obtain personal information from publicly available data sources outside of the bank system, which gave us complete access to the accounts. In addition, we developed an approach that bypassed the personal information requests for business accounts, which allowed us to log into these accounts. Once this was done we not only knew who owned the accounts, but we also got all of the other online capabilities for the accounts.

All experiments in this study were conducted using a Java application that disguised itself as the bank's applet. Therefore, no particular exploits using HTML forms were studied. However, most or all of the attacks described for the applet would also work with HTML forms. It is also possible to explore vulnerabilities that are particular to HTML forms, such as JavaScript attacks in older browsers. This access redundancy, which again was done for user-friendliness, is another weakness of the system, since it enables an attacker to explore flaws found, or to be found, in both HTML forms and Java applets. The attacker can then attack the subset of the clients that use that type of access.

This experiment made the tradeoff between user-friendliness and security very clear. In an attempt to give informative answers to users the application disclosed security relevant information. This flaw was present at several points in the banking application. Banking application developers should be very careful in deciding the type of diagnostic messages returned to the users in case of errors. Messages should be informative but should also be generic enough not to allow an attacker to determine what part of a set of submitted data is the cause of the error.

This chapter did not discuss possible denial of service attacks, either against the banking application (e.g., lockouts, flooding), or against the communication infrastructure (e.g., crashing of essential services, distributed denial of service). Recent attacks against major Internet sites [Dittrich, 1999] showed that these attacks are very difficult to block and that application designers should take into consideration the possibility of service disruptions.

Notes

1. This is a variation of the well known value checked vs. value used security problem [Bisbey et al., 1975].

References

[Bellovin, 1990] Bellovin, S. (1990). Security Problems in the TCP/IP Protocol Suite. *Computer Communications Review*, 19(2).

[Bisbey et al., 1975] Bisbey, R., Popek, G., and Carlstadt, J. (1975). Inconsistency of a Single Data Value Over Time. Technical Report ISI/SR-75-4, USC Information Sciences Institute.

[Dean et al., 1996] Dean, D., Felten, E., and Wallach, D. (1996). Security: From HotJava to Netscape and Beyond. In *Proceedings of the IEEE Symposium on Security and Privacy*. http://www.cs.princeton.edu/sip/pub/secure96.html.

[Dittrich, 1999] Dittrich, D. (1999). The DoS Project's "trinoo" distributed denial of service attack tool. http://staff.washington.edu/dittrich/misc/ddos/.

[dos Santos, 1997] dos Santos, A. (1997). Another way to exploit local classes in Java. Risks 19.41.

[Freier et al., 1996] Freier, A., Karlton, P., and Kocher, P. (1996). The SSL Protocol Version 3.0. INTERNET-DRAFT.

[Ghosh, 1998] Ghosh, A. K. (1998). *E-Commerce Security: Weak Links, Best Defenses*. John Wiley and Sons.

[Lindholm and Yellin, 1999] Lindholm, T. and Yellin, F. (1999). *The Java Virtual Machine Specification*. Addison-Wesley, 2nd edition.

[Paoli et al., 1998] Paoli, F. D., dos Santos, A., and Kemmerer, R. (1998). *Web Browsers and Security*, volume 1419 of *Lecture Notes in Computer Science*, pages 235–256. Springer-Verlag.

Chapter 2

SOFTWARE SECURITY ANALYSIS: AN EXAMPLE CASE STUDY

Brad Arkin

Cigital, Inc.
21351 Ridgetop Circle, Suite 400
Dulles, VA 20166
barkin@cigital.com

Abstract   This chapter presents an example outlining the process and results of a software security risk analysis. Unlike other types of security risk analyses, a software security analysis focuses on the design and implementation of the online application rather than the network and physical environment in which the application is deployed. An example is used to illustrate the benefits of a software security risk analysis and demonstrate how software security extends and complements conventional security and business risk analyses.

1.   Introduction

Software has become the dominant component in today's online systems. While at one point individuals may have been able to comprehend the intricacies of how software interacted with its operating environment, this is no longer the case for current e-commerce systems. Software development of online systems is not only marked by its large base of source code, but also by reliance on third party software component libraries and other commercial off the shelf components such as databases, servers, and operating system environments. Even simple flaws in programming can have dramatic effects on system security and reliability. The Year 2000 bug underscored the importance of software to modern systems and the expense and difficulty of analyzing and fixing software today, even for a relatively unsophisticated software bug.

The practice of traditional security risk assessment has not kept pace with the rapid changes to the critical role that software plays in overall system security. Most security risk assessment methodologies fail to address the software risks in the overall system. Risk assessment frameworks such as the ones described in [Craft, et al., 1998] and [Meritt, 1999] fail to address the complexity of software and its cornerstone role to the system. Software in modern systems demands special consideration compared to other system components with known and predictable failure modes.

The complexity of software and its critical role in e-commerce systems demands an in-depth analysis to properly understand and address the security risks introduced to a system by its software. This kind of software security risk analysis is described here in this case study. A software security risk analysis involves familiar risk analysis steps of identifying security risks and proposing mitigating strategies to balance functional needs against the system's security requirements; however the approach is tailored to meet the needs of current software development practices. When used in conjunction with a traditional security risk analysis, the software security risk analysis addresses the complex role of modern software in contemporary systems.

While the process described here is not confidential, the results from the analysis are always treated as client confidential. As a result, we depict a fictitious company named *SampleCasino.com* in this case study. The security risk analysis performed on SampleCasino.com's flagship casino poker game is patterned loosely after an independent analysis conducted on real online e-commerce sites. (See [Arkin, et al., 1999] for more.) Thus, while the client is fictitious, the application is not.

Section 2 describes the fictional client and the environment in which the software security analysis is performed. Section 3 details the data gathering phase of the process. Section 4 explains the analysis of the collected information and Section 5 presents the reporting process. Section 6 contains some concluding remarks.

2.   The client

SampleCasino.com's core group of developer/founders has expanded to include developers and development managers with much more experience and training in the finer points of software development. For a variety of reasons, including customer concerns, past security exploits, and the desire of new managers to better understand the product they are inheriting, these companies set out to perform an internal security risk assessment of their product and its operation.

In performing their internal security risk assessment SampleCasino .com identifies several areas as potential security problems. These issues and the associated mitigating steps taken are listed below:

- Lack of documented security policy — The operation and maintenance of the SampleCasino.com server and associated system administration tasks are undocumented and run largely on an ad hoc basis. There is no defined security policy to guide the system administrators or developers. To address this problem the management staff initiates the documentation of the operating procedures and the creation of a system-wide security policy. A system of quarterly reviews is established to ensure relevancy and accuracy of these documents in the future.

- Inadequate network security infrastructure — The SampleCasino. com corporate network infrastructure was built as the company grew, without a coherent plan of standardized configuration of machines and firewalls. To address this problem an outside contractor specializing in network security is brought in to perform an initial external security audit and provide security information and future audits to ensure the network security infrastructure is sound.

- Concerns about application security — The SampleCasino.com flagship casino poker game was designed and implemented with time to market driving the development schedule and system requirements. With no security expertise on staff and poor documentation of the current product, SampleCasino.com has no way of determining the nature and extent of the security risks imposed on the business by their own code. To address this issue, Sample-Casino.com requires a software security risk analysis.

3.   Data gathering

An optimal setting for performing a software security analysis includes system-wide documentation as well as documents detailing the security-critical components of the system. A list of the system's security requirements rounds out the set of documents necessary at the project's start. Unfortunately, the constraints of the new economy all too often lead to a development environment that considers requirements, specifications, documentation, and a defined development process to be extravagant luxuries beyond the means of a struggling start-up. Due to these constraints, the process of learning about a product such as SampleCasino.com's casino poker game is not as simple as collecting a stack of documentation and configuring a test system.

The lack of good documentation yields a data gathering process divided into two phases. The first phase includes a preliminary investigation into the company and the product through the limited information gained during the pre-sales effort and online resources. The goal of this initial phase is to develop a rudimentary knowledge of the product under review, the terminology used by the company, and the marketing claims about the product.

Following the completion of this initial step, a team of security analysts make an on-site visit to meet with developers and management to learn about the product and its implementation in detail. The goal of the on-site visit is to acquire as much information as possible about the product and the surrounding security issues. Meetings with the business manager for the product are important to understand what is most valuable to the company from a business perspective, while meetings with the technical staff provide insight into the inner workings of the product. This understanding of the business and technical issues surrounding the product is critical in making the best risk management decisions involving the tricky tradeoffs between security and business objectives.

The two data gathering phases are explained in the following sections.

3.1.   Preliminary investigation

Information can be gained from initial phone interviews and online through Internet research. By paging through the SampleCasino.com website as well as several different Internet gambling and casino poker discussion forums and newsgroups, the following information is learned about their new product:

- SampleCasino.com's product appears to be the first online poker game that allows anyone with an Internet connection to compete against each other (as opposed to the House) in real-time for real money. SampleCasino.com first went live with their casino poker game nearly two years ago.

- Users are required to register with SampleCasino.com using a valid credit card and the corresponding billing address so that winnings and losses can be dealt with accordingly.

- The product has a fat client-server architecture that supports the Windows NT platform.

- Upon successful registration, users are given an account with a username/password pair that is required upon starting each new poker session.

- The casino software developed by SampleCasino.com has been licensed to several other online casinos, however, according to online discussion groups, SampleCasino.com consistently draws the best crowds.

3.2.   On-site visit

Following the preliminary investigation, the on-site portion of the analysis begins. The goal of this initial meeting is to learn the basic concept of operations for the system and to understand the underlying system design. The chief architect of the casino poker game provides a white board level description of the software architecture and design. This quickly develops into a freewheeling discussion in which both the security analysts and SampleCasino.com developers ask many questions, some of which cannot be answered definitively. At times the Sample-Casino.com development team discusses amongst itself fairly low-level issues such as how the passwords are stored in the database.

All available project documentation is provided to the analysts. In addition, a chart mapping each of the SampleCasino.com developers to the components of the casino poker game each one knows best is created. The rest of the first day is spent experimenting with a test system of the casino poker game to learn the capabilities and limitations of the system. The analysts read through the documentation collected during the kickoff meeting and make note of any discrepancies with the earlier discussion.

The notes and questions recorded during the kickoff meeting and the subsequent testing of and reading about the product are used to highlight questions and issues to investigate. The questions used to probe the developers are derived in part from discussion and in part from a database of questions, problems, and issues for similar Internet-based client-server systems. This master set of questions has been developed over time based on the results of many software security risk analyses and from research findings. This set of questions regarding the design and implementation details of the product are used to ensure a complete and thorough analysis of each product reviewed. Some sample questions from this list are:

- What tools are used to support code revisions, testing, and other development tasks?

- How are passwords, credit card information and other user-specific data stored in the database?

- Is there a privacy policy in place? How is this supported by the architecture?

- How is the communication between the client and the server encrypted?

- How is each message authenticated?

- What key negotiation protocol is used?

- Where are random numbers used in the system? How are these values generated?

- Exactly what audit information is logged in the database? How is this audit information accessed and used?

Using the set of questions as a starting point, the individual discussions with each developer also follow the loose format of the kickoff meeting. Developers will frequently contradict each others' statements. As a result of these inconsistencies, source code must be reviewed to serve as the final determinant as to how certain parts of the system are implemented.

4.   Analysis

Armed with a hefty stack of source listings, documentation, and notes, the security analyst team returns to their site to begin the analysis of the data collected during the SampleCasino.com on-site visit. An initial meeting is used to ground the analysis on a firm starting point and spawns independent investigations by team members into open questions and issues. These independent investigations are identified during the kickoff meeting and assigned to team members based on their domain expertise. Once all open issues have been fully investigated, the team reconvenes to discuss the identified risks and propose mitigation strategies to improve the overall security of the system. The entire analysis phase takes two to three weeks.

This process is described below.

4.1.   Kickoff meeting

The kickoff meeting at the home base follows the same format as the one held at SampleCasino.com. The team lead presents the product architecture at the white-board level and then proceeds to drill down into the more interesting issues pointing out potential problems along the way. Debate occurs frequently as the different team members use the notes and source code collected during the on-site visit to verify key points. Throughout the meeting, one of the white-boards in the room is used to track all open questions and issues that require further investigation. These questions concern the design and implementation of the system's security critical components. In some cases, clear risks in the system are identified during this internal kickoff meeting.

Some of the issues and questions noted during this meeting are listed below:

- Is the shuffling algorithm sound?

- How are the random values used to drive the shuffling algorithm generated?

- What is being done with the logged audit data?

- No encryption is used to protect client-server communication.

- All information in the database, including passwords and credit card numbers, is stored in clear text.

- There are no strong user password enforcement mechanisms.

- The SampleCasino.com privacy policy is currently not supported by any technical features.

Once all of the collected material has been reviewed, the meeting concludes with the assignment of the open questions and identified risks to different members of the team. This is done according to the individual strengths of the team members as well as each one's interest and familiarity with particular aspects of the system. For instance, the issues surrounding card shuffling and pseudo-random number generation are given to the most mathematically inclined member of the team while the problems of retrofitting the system with encryption capabilities are assigned to the crypto enthusiast.

4.2.   Investigation

Each team member leaves the analysis kickoff meeting with a set of questions and known problems in the product. The goal of each team member during the investigation phase is to determine definitive answers on any remaining open questions and also to produce one or more potential mitigation strategies for the identified risks. This process follows the path of any small research task: the investigator pulls from past experiences and various information resources available on the Internet or contained in the corporate knowledge base to develop answers and solutions to the issues at hand. The corporate knowledge base is particularly useful during this investigation due to the fact that there are classes of security bugs (such as buffer overflows in C/C++) that are repeatedly implemented in commercial software that have been identified in previous software risk analyses, and as a result have been included in the knowledge base.

Using the set of math-related tasks as an example, a given team member begins by using the web and simulation textbooks to learn more about card shuffling algorithms. The analyst soon determines that the algorithm used by SampleCasino.com to shuffle the deck of cards prior to each hand of the casino poker game is an off-by-one implementation of a flawed algorithm that does not produce a uniform distribution of decks even when supplied a statistically random source of numbers. In the course of this research, the widely used algorithm that does produce a uniform distribution of decks is identified and recorded. The next issue to investigate is the random number generator used to drive the card shuffling algorithm. After several dead-ends and a couple false leads, a newsgroup posting reveals the answer: The Delphi random number generator used by SampleCasino.com is a standard 32-bit linear congruential number generator seeded by default with the number of milliseconds since midnight GMT according to the system clock. The analyst verifies this with an experimental program and begins to develop some potential solutions for SampleCasino.com to use for mitigating this problem.

The problems involving random number generation is one of the most common vulnerabilities in security critical software. This is an area where poor developer training and the misuse of tools meant for use in stochastic simulation introduces potential problems. The lack of a cryptographically secure random number generator in software for the Windows NT platform is another contributing factor in making this such a widespread problem. A frequently referenced instance of this problem is the weak generation of SSL session keys in early versions of Netscape. (For more see [Goldberg and Wagner, 1996].)

Throughout the course of this work on the random number generation issue the team member also interacts frequently with other members on the team. Using informal hallway discussions and white board sessions, the team members are able to pull from a wide array of expertise and experience in attacking the problems at hand.

4.3. Risk mitigation

The team re-groups once all of the team members have completed their assigned tasks from the analysis kickoff meeting. With a few more members in attendance to provide outside opinions, each team member reviews the problems encountered, describes the identified risks, and proposes a mitigation strategy. These meetings are rarely litanies of identified risks and their corresponding mitigation strategies, but rather lively discussions that serve to integrate the findings of the independent analyses into a comprehensive system-wide software risk analysis.

One by one the identified risks are brought up and discussed. In most cases the mitigation strategies developed prior to the meeting merely serve as starting points for debate and discussion that yield a final result. The goal of this discussion is to not only develop appropriate mitigation strategies to address the risks, but also to categorize and rank the risks according to the specific issues important to the client. The discussion of potential mitigation strategies and the ranking of risks focuses on the tradeoffs between increased security and the business objectives of the client. The team lead is responsible for keeping the discussion grounded in the issues that are most important to the client.

Sometimes several individual problems are solved together in one fell swoop with the use of broad design change. In other cases only minor changes in small components are required. Below are examples of the mitigation strategies agreed upon for some of the identified risks in SampleCasino.coms casino poker game. These risks are ranked according to the order in which they should be addressed by the SampleCasino.com development team.

- Card shuffling — Replace the card shuffling algorithm with the new one providing a statistically even distribution. Also, replace the Delphi Random() function with a secure random number generation method such as the outputs of a securely seeded stream cipher. The implementation details involved in mitigating this risk are tricky, so analysts will have to work closely with the development team at SampleCasino.com to ensure that it is done correctly.

- Architectural support for privacy policy — Use technology to enforce the claims made by SampleCasino.com in the privacy policy. To ensure that the user credit card information will never be accessed without the express consent of the card owner, the credit card information must be encrypted. To prevent even the SampleCasino.com system administrators from having offline access to the encryption keys used each credit card number should be encrypted with a key constructed from the clear text of the user's password. Although the loss of a user password will require the reentry of the credit card information, SampleCasino.com is eager to implement this feature due to the security conscious image it helps present.

- Lack of client-server encryption — Use a standard SSL library to secure the currently unencrypted communication channel.

- Clear text password storage — Use a widely deployed hash algorithm such as SHA-1 along with a small salt value (A salt is two or more random characters that are stored in the clear in the database along with the hash value.) instead of storing passwords in clear text. (For more on this, see [Schneier, 1996].)

5.   Results

For a fast-moving company such as SampleCasino.com the development managers place a large emphasis on time-to-market. As a result, the best way for the analysts to present the results of their security risk analysis of their product is to provide an on-site visit to supplement the written report documenting each discovered risk, its potential impact, and proposed mitigation strategy. The team returns to SampleCasino.com to spend a day on-site with the development team making sure they understand the problems and buy into the proposed solutions.

The on-site visit begins with a morning presentation. The team lead goes through the identified risks, grouped according to categories such as authentication, database issues, and random number generation. The development staff and managers from SampleCasino.com follow along with printouts of the slides and notes prepared by the analysts prior to the visit. Each issue is introduced, discussed, and assigned to a particular developer. Frequently the discussion moves to a white board for better illustrating the issue at hand.

Team members meet individually with the developers who have been assigned engineering tasks and work with them to review the problems and proposed solutions. Occasionally further issues crop up which are discussed and incorporated into a modified risk mitigation strategy, but for the most part these meetings are straightforward and conclude quickly. The goal is that by the end of the day each of the identified risks have been mitigated with a reasonable solution that is owned by a particular developer at SampleCasino.com. This sense of ownership in implementing the fix is crucial for ensuring that the changes actually make their way into real code.

Following the on-site visit, the team will compose a short write-up detailing each of the specific engineering tasks that were developed during the on-site presentation of results. The audience of the report is the development manager. The goal is for the development manager to be able to incorporate these tasks and follow up with the appropriate developers to make sure that they have completed the work. For each engineering task, a description of the work to be done, a listing of the risk this work will mitigate, and the developer assigned is included. Examples of these engineering tasks are:

- Password handling — The passwords are currently stored in the database in clear text, allowing anyone with database access to compromise all user passwords. This risk should be mitigated by first hashing the user password using SHA-1 along with a prepended salt. When authenticating a user, the supplied password with the prepended salt is first hashed and then compared to the value stored in the database. We discussed this issue with Raul S. and he is in charge of this task.

- Client-server communication — The communication channel between the client and the server is currently unencrypted. This exposes SampleCasino.com to a large number of risks. Using a standard SSL library to establish a secure channel for communication prior to any other client-server communication should mitigate these risks. Once the SSL connection is established, the standard client-server communication can proceed unchanged. We discussed this issue with David Z. and he is in charge of this task.

During the execution of these engineering tasks, the team remains available to the developers to help with any problems or hidden details. This is normally done via email or phone calls. For a simple system such as the casino poker game there is no need for an additional on-site visit. The engineering tasks are generally completed within a week or two after the presentation of results. The analysts ensure these changes are appropriate responses to the identified risks through additional reviews of the newly updated source code. After these security reviews, the new code is handed off to SampleCasino.com for Quality Assurance and Reliability testing. These changes often reach production within the month.

6.   Conclusions

This case study presents a sample software security risk analysis of SampleCasino.com's casino poker game. The security analyst team followed their standard process in performing this analysis and the results were similar to the security risk analyses performed for other first time clients. This process involved gathering data about the design and implementation of the system, the identification of software risks, the development of mitigation strategies to address these risks, and the reporting of results back to the client. By following the analysis with rapid feedback and strong technical support to the SampleCasino.com development staff the team was able to facilitate real changes in the product that raised the overall level of security.

The software security risk analysis provided a much stronger response to the risks posed by the systems' software than the performing only the broader security risk analysis of the entire SampleCasino.com operation of the casino poker game. By applying software security expertise in the analysis of the SampleCasino.com poker game, the best understanding of the risks posed by the software to the security of the system was gained. The importance of the software in a business system such as the casino poker game run by SampleCasino.com requires that the appropriate software security expertise is used to identify and mitigate the software security risks to the system. By supplementing the standard risk analysis with the software security analysis the overall understanding and mitigation of the security risks is greatly improved.

References

[Arkin, et al., 1999] Arkin, B., Hill, F., Marks, S., McGraw, G., Schmid M., and Walls, T. "How We Learned to Cheat at Online Poker: A Study in Software Security." *Developer.com: Tech Focus,* (September 28, 1999).

[Craft, et al., 1998] Craft, R., Wyss, G., Vandewart, R., and Funkhouser, D. "An Open Framework for Risk Management." *Proc. 21rst NISSC* (1998).

[Goldberg and Wagner, 1996] Goldberg, I. and Wagner, D. "Randomness and the Netscape Browser." *Dr. Dobbs Journal,* (January, 1996.)

[Meritt, 1999] Meritt, J. "A Method for Quantitative Risk Analysis." *Proc. 22nd NISSC* (1999).

[Meritt, 1998] Meritt, J. "Risk Management." *Proc. 21rst NISSC* (1998).

[Schneier, 1996] Schneier, B. *Applied Cryptography (Second Edition).* John Wiley and Sons, 1996.

Chapter 3

NEW SECURITY ISSUES IN MOBILE E-COMMERCE

Anup K. Ghosh

Cigital, Inc.
21351 Ridgetop Circle, #400
Dulles, VA 20166
anup.ghosh@computer.org

Abstract   By 2004, there is expected to be over 1 billion wireless device sub-scribers. The future of e-commerce appears to be headed straight for mobile e-commerce (m-commerce). Today's workers want to be un-tethered from their desktops with the freedom to communicate with anyone, anywhere, anytime. To this end, current wireless platforms are integrating voice telephony, data, and streaming multimedia in multi-function rich-content capable devices. In the future, code will be ex-changed transparently with data over wireless links. Wireless devices will have the processing power and memory of today's desktop worksta-tions. Wireless devices will have direct connections to file servers and network services behind the corporate firewalls. Furthermore, wireless devices will have the ability to ship and execute mobile and itinerant code such as software agents that act on the user's behalf. The security and privacy concerns are paramount for consumers and businesses. In this chapter, we describe the key security concerns in mobile e-commerce and avenues for addressing them.

1.   Mobile Commerce — The Next Generation of E-Commerce

E-commerce, or using the Internet to conduct business for commercial or personal purposes, has proven to be the driving force in the new economy. It is expected that e-commerce related business will reach one-third of the US gross domestic product within five years. E-commerce is expected to hit US $6 trillion in sales by 2004 in just business-to-business (B2B) transactions. Internet-based transactions expect to make up 25 percent of all retail transactions in the next decade.

Today, e-commerce is mostly conducted from the desktop using workstations and personal computers. Tomorrow, we expect that a significant portion of e-commerce will be conducted from wireless, Internet-enabled devices. Wireless devices will provide users mobility to research, communicate, and purchase goods and services from anywhere at anytime without being tethered to the desktop. Using the Internet from wireless devices has come to be known as mobile e-commerce, or simply m-commerce, and encompasses far many activities beyond online purchasing. One of the major wireless applications is Web access for research and real-time information retrieval such as weather, maps, and stock quotes. E-mail will continue to dominate online applications. Innovative online applications, which for instance, use location reference of end users, will drive forward new areas of e-commerce. In fact, both new and older applications being ported to wireless devices will provide further growth impetus to online commerce and is likely to render current estimates for e-commerce growth overly conservative.

Currently, there are over 385,000 wireless Internet subscribers (Strategis Group). By 2004, there are expected to be over 1 billion wireless device users, some 600 million wireless Internet subscribers, and a US $200 billion mobile e-commerce market. The average cost per minute of wireless usage is expected to drop down to US 2 cents per minute in 2004 [Zerega, 1999]. It is expected that by 2008, the number of wireless Internet devices will outnumber wired devices [Lewis, 1999]. While these estimates will likely change wildly in the coming months and years, there is clearly a vast number of current wireless device subscribers worldwide, and a large number of future potential wireless Internet subscribers and applications. Mobile e-commerce will only drive the growth of wireless devices and applications. However, securing mobile e-commerce will be essential in order to unleash the potentially very large mobile e-commerce market. Consumers appear to be very wary of security and privacy issues particularly in wireless devices since the ease of snooping wireless conversations is better understood than snooping data packets on land lines.

M-commerce will be conducted using a variety of devices such as mobile phones, pagers, hand-held personal digital assistants (PDAs) such as Palm Computing's Palm Organizer and Microsoft's PocketPC, and sub-notebooks, and wireless notebooks. Furthermore, it is likely that appliances in 300 million US homes, 45 million cars, and other countless non-traditional computing devices will become wireless Internet-enabled in the next decade, making desktop Internet access a relic of the past [Lewis, 1999]. Vendors have been promoting novel applications of m-commerce such as paying at cash registers, parking meters, vending machines, and ticket booths. However, in truth, wireless devices will take on all the functionality of today's desktop machines and more.

As the form factor of mobile computing devices has gotten smaller, the computing capacity has grown significantly. Today's hand-held devices have equivalent computing power as their desktop computing counterparts of one generation earlier. This phenomenon, while driving more and more functionality into hand-held wireless Internet-enabled devices, also is driving security risks we have today in desktop computing into wireless devices. For example, malicious code, long a problem in desktop computing, is likely to be a problem in hand-held devices before long. In this chapter, new security risks in wireless mobile computing are examined from a risk-oriented analysis.

2. Mobile E-Commerce Security

Most industry analysts agree that security and privacy in mobile e-commerce will be critical for widespread adoption. Any perceived lack of privacy will deter consumers from making online purchases from wireless devices, or from using location-oriented commerce applications that transmit individual users' locations to remote sites. Currently, many consumers are acutely aware that their cordless phone and cell phone conversations can be eavesdropped at will by curious neighbors with a scanner. Most consumers know that their phone number, by default, are transmitted to the other party with their phone call. Some might consider this a convenience for ordering delivery food, some a benefit of knowing who is calling before picking up the phone, and others an invasion of privacy. These perceptions in older generation wireless devices will impact the way users adopt m-commerce applications unless privacy concerns are addressed forthrightly up front.

The very reasons businesses are beginning to adopt wireless devices as part of the corporate IT infrastructure are giving rise to security concerns over wireless computing. For businesses, full enterprise integration with application, file, and network servers behind the corporate firewall is a major driving force for widespread adoption of wireless devices. Where the Palm Pilots appealed to individuals for organizing personal appointments, enterprise-enabled wireless companions are more likely to appeal to businesses because of the ability to wirelessly synchronize mail and contacts, the ability to read, write, and exchange desktop application documents, and to use full-featured Web browsers. Many handheld PCs now come equipped with modems that allow devices to dial into corporate intranets. Some provide built-in support for wireless Local Area

Network (LAN) access. The H/PC Pro supports wireless connections to Ethernet networks using IEEE 802.11 wireless LAN standard.

The security risks for businesses in integrating wireless devices into their corporate infrastructure are significant. The problem is best understood by the weak link in the chain analogy. The security of the corporate infrastructure is only as strong as its weakest link. With fixed (wired) devices, system administrators have some measure of control over the infrastructure. With a large number of wireless mobile devices connecting inside and outside the network, access to resources must be carefully controlled. This will require authentication, confidentiality, and authorization mechanisms. Even more, new risks posed by wireless devices will require strong software security mechanisms to ensure safe behavior, appropriate access control mechanisms, and to detect and prevent proliferation of malicious software.

In addition to contending with the usual Internet security threats in online applications, wireless devices introduce new hazards specific to their mobility and communication medium. For instance, wireless devices can form ad hoc networks where a collection of peer mobile nodes communicate with each other without assistance from a fixed infrastructure [Zhang and Lee, 2000]. One implication of ad hoc networks is that network decision making is decentralized. As a result, network protocols tend to rely on cooperation between all participating nodes. An adversary can exploit this vulnerability to compromise cooperative algorithms. For instance, ad hoc wireless routing protocols are cooperative in nature [Royer and Toh, 1999]. An adversary that compromises a single node can disseminate false routing information to take down the ad hoc network, or worse, instruct all routing to go through the compromised node [Zhang and Lee, 2000].

Similarly, mobile users will roam through many different cells, ad hoc networks, administrative boundaries, and security domains. As the communication is handed off from one domain to the next, a single malicious or compromised domain can potentially compromise wireless devices through malicious downloads, misinformation, or simply deny service.

In summary, mobile and wireless devices will introduce new security and privacy risks to both consumers and businesses. Using wireless devices for m-commerce will result in new vulnerabilities and potentially a new weak link in e-commerce [Ghosh, 1998]. Since attackers tend to exploit the weakest link in the chain, the security risks of wireless devices must be carefully analyzed and addressed. In this chapter, new risks in mobile e-commerce are described.

3.   Security Risks in Mobile Commerce

Vendors of wireless devices and systems are beginning to promote their products as the secure mobile e-commerce solution. Before buying the marketing literature, it is important to understand the risks involved in m-commerce transactions. In this chapter, technology risks in m-commerce are examined by highlighting weak links in each of the different component technologies involved in m-commerce transactions. The security of m-commerce systems is only as strong as its weakest link. In practice, we find that hackers tend to attack weak links rather than waste time on the harder problems. Therefore, an effective risk management strategy is to identify weak links, and make these stronger, thus making the effort at compromising m-commerce systems more difficult for would-be attackers.

In the rest of this chapter, weak links in the following components of m-commerce systems are examined: the wireless device, application software, the communication link, the server systems and related applications.

4.   The Wireless Device

The wireless device consists of hardware and software, each posing its own security and vulnerability properties. One characteristic often touted as a virtue is the small form factor hand-held devices have. The virtue is that because they are small, they can be kept on your person and personal (physical) security measures can be used to keep the devices secure. Another virtue is that because these devices tend not to be shared (either physically such as shared workstations) or logically (such as shared file systems, at least for the moment), they are relatively secure devices to store very confidential information such as private keys. However, the small form factor has its own risks. For instance, PDAs are often set down, lost, or stolen. Their small size makes it more easy to forget and to steal. As a result, very confidential information can be easily lost or stolen, creating potentially very big headaches with certificate revocation, and recovering other lost data.

Unfortunately, the perceived virtues of personal physical security may have been taken to heart too much by the manufacturers of the devices. As an example, the user authentication mechanisms on these devices installed by the manufacturers tend to be either trivially breakable or non-existent. As a result, if the device is stolen, the adversary will not have a very hard time logging in and gaining access to confidential data and applications.

The small form factor of the devices also places constraints on the amount of CPU cycles, memory, long-term storage, display, user input mechanism, and peripherals (such as modems) that can be installed with the device. One of the key risks with limited resources is that denial-of-service attacks that consume all available CPU, network bandwidth, and available memory are relatively easy to implement. Even inadvertent risks such as bandwidth-hungry applications can quickly bring wireless networks to their knees. Imagine Napster- and Gnutella–like programs downloading music files or software over wireless networks around the clock. Also, since handhelds are notoriously power hungry (particularly those with color displays), the user will often times run low on batteries. If the batteries have died completely, important data in volatile memory can be lost.

The small display size and limited bandwidth of PDAs limit the amount and type of information that can be physically displayed to the end user, necessitating special browsers or Web sites for "clipped" content. A small display size might pose unusual risks such as the user not seeing the full context of transactions if he or she is not aware that paging is needed. However, the fact that handhelds do have a display is a significant virtue over smartcards that might require connections with untrusted devices to display transactions. Unlike smartcards, if the wireless device is programmed accordingly, the device's display can be used to inform the user when transactions are taking place and particulars of the transactions, such as the amount of money exchanged.

The platform or operating system that the device runs is equally important to determining security risks. For instance, as of this writing, the Palm OS provides no memory protection for its applications [Balfanz and Felten, 1999]. This failing poses serious threats for each application's own security and privacy. For instance, a trusted application that uses a private key for signing documents can be attacked by a rogue application. The rogue application can attempt to steal the decrypted key in the signing application's memory by interrupting it at just the right time [Balfanz and Felten, 1999]. Other important operating system attributes include access control to files, the ability for untrusted entities to write programs to disk, differentiated privileges (*e.g.*, administrator vs. user), file sharing over networks, and the robustness and quality of operating system code.

To address these platform risks, the PDA operating system needs to enforce memory protection between applications to prevent one application from spying on another. The second fundamental protection necessary is access control for principals and objects to prevent unprivileged programs and users from accessing confidential data such as private keys or confidential information in databases. The operating system should also support encrypted tunnels or VPNs to provide confidential access over insecure wireless links. Finally, strong authentication mechanisms should be built in to authenticate the user to the device, such as fingerprint biometrics, or simply encrypting passwords.

5. Application Risks

Software applications that run on the platform pose considerable risks to the device and to m-commerce applications. The two significant risks with application software are malicious code and inadvertently flawed code.

5.1. Malicious code risks

Malicious code is software or code fragments intentionally written to corrupt system integrity, violate data confidentiality, or change program functionality without the knowledge and approval of the user [Bergeron et al., 1999].

Malicious code is becoming one of the most significant problems in Internet-based commerce. A study by Computer Economics of Carlsbad, CA, estimates that in the first two quarters of 1999 alone, businesses worldwide lost more than U.S $7.6 billion due to malicious code.

One of the key problems to containing malicious code is the problem of unauthorized software proliferation. The distribution of malicious software has been a problem for computer networks since the early days of electronic bulletin boards known as BBSs. BBSs were publicly accessible sites where you could post and download software freely. Even then, it was well-understood that untrusted software like those found on BBS sites could be potentially malicious. As a rule of thumb, any software downloaded from a BBS site was not to be installed on an organization's computer system. Rather, this software was mainly for personal use to be installed on personal computers at home.

The problem of malicious software has only grown since the days of BBSs. The BBS has been replaced with the Web and mobile code now seamlessly and sometimes silently downloads and executes on Web surfers' machines. With the rise of the personal computer in the 1980s, malicious code became best known in the form of viruses, which are self-replicating code snippets that can infect common programs. The most common vector for spreading viruses was the floppy which often infected the boot sector of the personal computer.

As the Internet became more pervasive and floppy disks less essential, viruses were spread via shared application documents in email. Macro viruses were invented to demonstrate that desktop applications can not only run code interactively (meaning the application was itself an interpreter), but also can run self-replicating code by infecting templates and subsequent working documents.

Now with the advent of wireless Internet access via PDAs, malicious code will have a new platform onto which to wreak havoc and spread. Some PDAs already offer the ability to exchange documents. Most provide the ability to download software from personal computers. Soon, most will be downloading program executables and active content in addition to Web data over wireless Internet connections.

Unknown programs, often times entertaining and clever diversions from work, are attached to emails and distributed widely inside and outside organizations. Users end up clicking on attachments and running programs for entertainment without knowing the full behavior of these programs. Many Trojan horses, as well as an equal number of hoaxes, are spread in this manner. Even users cognizant that executing untrusted programs can be dangerous can be fooled into executing programs. Some Trojan horse programs have been disguised as JPEG or GIF attachments when they are in fact program executables whose suffix appears to be .jpg or .gif. When launched, instead of getting an image, an error box is sometimes displayed (to dupe the user into believing some error occurred in displaying the graphic), while the Trojan installs itself and begins its havoc.

In addition to attachments, program executables are often downloaded from Web sites on public shareware/freeware sites or as mobile code (such as ActiveX controls). Corporations often frown on downloading and installing programs (to the point of writing company policies prohibiting downloading of software), however, in practice, they have little control over this activity. One reason is that users sometimes do not know they are downloading executables, such as in the case of mobile code that downloads and executes transparently. Secondly, because email attachments are used as part of the normal course of business, blocking attachments at the firewall is generally not an acceptable solution. Also, because an executable can be disguised as other kinds of documents, firewalling solutions have proven to be ineffective.

On the PDA or other wireless device, it is likely that code will be pushed to the user often without his or her consent. The user is less apt to use the device as a general purpose computer, and more apt to use the device to communicate and use online applications. As a result, many feature enhancements, upgrades, and even new software installs will be downloaded automatically without the user's knowledge or blessing, in order to make the experience less PC-like, and more appliance-like.

The push paradigm made its splash with PointCast on personal computers, but has become more subtle recently, embedding itself within operating systems with names like Active Desktop. Many software applications will automatically upgrade themselves either by scheduled pull or by vendor pushes of new patches and release versions to their installed subscriber base. While leaving the user out of the loop as far as downloading and installing software makes software more usable and dynamic, it also poses serious risks by providing a new vector for malicious software to automatically download, install, and run.

In many current and future m-commerce applications, digital signing of documents or transactions will be an essential component, both for establishing authenticity of principals, as well as providing non-repudiation in transactions. In the future, courts may consider digital signatures on documents to hold the legal weight and authority of hand-written signatures on physical documents. Malicious software can compromise this system by signing documents on the user's behalf without the user's knowledge. Doing so is relatively easy. In many browsers and mailers that support signing, passphrases that unlock private keys for signing are cached by design for ease of use. Malicious software can use the cached passphrase to sign documents without the signatory's knowledge. If digital signatures are legally binding, this can cause legal liability for actions the user did not perform. Even without cached passphrases, most passphrases can be decrypted from non-volatile RAM by DES key attacks or by dictionary attacks against login PINs and passwords.

Disclosure of confidential documents or data is one of the most salient risks of malicious software. The user has little observability or control over which data is sent out over the wireless connection. If the malicious software cannot perform a DES key attack on the device itself, it can send the encrypted private key out to an adversary site for offline decryption.

Malicious software also undermines confidentiality provided by encryption protocols and VPNs. When establishing a secure online connection between the wireless device and a server, the data is decrypted typically at the server gateway and at the data reader (*e.g.*, browser or mailer) on the device. At either end of the connection, the encrypted data is decrypted and stored in plain text in non-volatile RAM or disk. Rather than attempting to break the secure channel, an adversary need only compromise the device (or the gateway or server) to gain access to the confidential data in clear text. Malicious software serves this purpose well. A malicious applet or executable that is downloaded (or pushed) to the device can read confidential data in plain text and send it out over the wireless link (even over an encrypted channel!) to the adversary's site.

To provide protection against malicious code risks, install filters should be built into wireless device platforms such that software cannot automatically install and run without the user's knowledge. Furthermore, software should carry digital certificates of authenticity that vouch not only for the author or publisher of the software, but also for the integrity of the software such that the end user will know it has not been corrupted. The user will be required then to approve of all requested new software installations and upgrades.

Clearly, there will also be a role for anti-viral products to run on PDAs as well. The key problem with anti-viral products, however, is that they are largely signature-based. These products are excellent at identifying and eradicating known viruses, however, they fail to identify new threats. Since virus infections now spread at the speed of the Internet, PDAs will need additional protection mechanisms. One possible solution is to disable many types of active content by default. Users who wish to run active content such as Java applets, Java scripts, VBScripts can do so at their own risk, and for selected sites and selected emails only. Another option is to provide protective havens or sandboxes in which untrusted content can safely run, while barring access to trusted portions of the device such as working directories and privileged system calls. Finally, there will a role for host-based intrusion detection to detect anomalous behavior on the device. These forward-looking solutions will address not only known malicious code threats, but also future unknown threats to the user and to m-commerce in general.

5.2. Software flaws

The other serious category of application risks is in flawed software. Most computer security violations in practice are made by exploiting flawed software. For instance, roughly 50 percent of the CERT Coordination Center's alerts from 1998-99 are related to inadvertent software flaws.

As the market for PDA application software heats up, more and more applications will be available for the most popular platforms such as the Palm OS, EPOC, and Windows CE. The more ubiquitous a particular platform becomes, the greater the software base will be, and the more likely the platform will be threatened with application-based attacks.

The most pervasive software flaw is the buffer overrun flaw. This flaw is created when the software developer fails to check the length of incoming input buffers before copying the buffer to a stack frame variable. The result is that an attacker able to exploit a buffer overrun flaw can run arbitrary code on the machine, often times with super user privileges. Most buffer overrun flaws occur in programs written in unsafe languages such as C, which do not perform type checking. PDAs are a prime risk because the development languages for these platforms tend to be C or even assembly. A safer language for wireless application development would be a type-safe language such as Java. Sun Microsystems Java Platform 2, Micro Edition, is expected to be available for the Palm operating system in the future.

Traditionally, most application-based attacks are launched against servers, rather than the client systems. However, in m-commerce transactions, the client software may be the target of malicious servers. For instance, a malicious server will attempt to gain information about the client, such as type of platform, user, email address, and any software version numbers to reveal potential vulnerabilities. Furthermore, mobile code or active content applications are likely to play a large part in m-commerce transactions. Many attacks against mobile code applications are against the mobile code interpreter, which will typically run in the browser. Thus, a server may attempt to overrun buffers in a PDA browser, an applet may attempt to break type safety, or an active script may attempt to crash its interpreter. Once code is involved in exploiting software flaws, the problem really goes back to the malicious code problem discussed in the preceding section.

Finally, as PDAs are given more and more horsepower, they will likely become servers in some fashion, whether it is to act as a server for distributed applications, as a mail or FTP server, or even a Web server. The H/PC Pro companion can already run FTP, TFTP, and Web server software. Host-based intrusion detection approaches can play an important role in detecting attacks against these services.

6.   Communication Link Risks

Much work has been performed in communications security over the last several decades, starting with information theory, and including the latest advances in elliptic curve cryptography. In spite the maturity of the field, wireless devices pose new and significant threats to m-commerce because of the nature of the communication medium they use. By and large, most of the threats to m-commerce will not be solved by encryption.

The nature of wireless networks makes them vulnerable to attack. Each wireless device serves as its own node in ad hoc dynamic networks. Mobile devices are autonomous units that roam from network to network. Unlike fixed wire networks, in wireless ad hoc networks, the physical network need not be attacked, nor is there a fixed network infrastructure that can be physically protected with bricks and locks or logically protected with firewalls and gateways.

Rather than an attacker needing to pursue a target, targets can come to attackers in wireless networks simply by roaming through the attacker's zone. Wireless devices pass through many different untrusted networks from which service is derived and data is exchanged. Information can be stolen or altered without the end user knowing any better. Service can be, and is often, easily denied, inadvertently or not. Transactions can be interrupted, then re-instated, often without re-authenticating principals. Request can be re-directed and malicious code can be surreptitiously downloaded together with expected Web data.

As users roam through various untrusted networks, which by virtue of cooperative protocols must be trusted, connections are handed off from one zone to another. During hand-offs, connections may be interrupted mid-transaction. Simply "re-freshing" a browser to re-establish the connection may inadvertently introduce risks. For instance, the new zone may be a malicious one that re-establishes a connection not with the intended principal, but with a malicious entity whose purpose it is to capture account and password information. Re-establishing connections and transactions without authenticating principals on both sides of the transactions can be dangerous. Most Web sites currently are not configured to deal with intermittent service failures as is common to wireless connections. Most vendor implementations of SSL do not re-authenticate principals or re-check certificates once a connection has been established within the current session. Attackers can use this vulnerability to their advantage in wireless networks.

The wireless network is ripe for man-in-the-middle attacks, well-known to fixed wire Internet. In man-in-the-middle attacks, an attacker will interpose their site or service between the end user and the intended destination site. Often times, the attacker's site will give the look and feel of the intended site. For instance, if the user were to check CNNfn regularly for stock quotes in and around airports, a malicious user can alter directory naming services (DNS) in ad hoc networks around the airport to re-direct all CNNfn requests to their site. Since secure DNS is still not implemented and deployed in practice, it is not very difficult to compromise the DNS, simply by establishing your own DNS server that other people necessarily trust. Providing the same look and feel of a Web site is easy since it can be duplicated perfectly simply by downloading the site. The insidious part of the attack is in discreetly changing dynamic information — such as stock quotes — to benefit the malicious entity.

As mentioned earlier, many ad hoc wireless protocols use cooperative algorithms that rely on cooperative participation of all nodes in the network [Zhang and Lee, 2000]. Decision making in ad hoc wireless networks is decentralized and largely requires cooperation and trust between member nodes. Wireless ad hoc networks consist of a collection of peer mobile nodes that communicate directly with each other via wireless links without assistance from a fixed infrastructure [Zhang and Lee, 2000]. Nodes far apart use intermediate nodes to serve as relays and to provide routing. Thus, all nodes function as routers that discover and maintain routes between member nodes. This functionality is handled at the network layer of the wireless protocol and is transparent to the wireless applications.

In this trusted and cooperative model, a single malicious node can compromise the integrity of the whole network. For instance, the media access control (MAC) protocols of wireless networks are vulnerable to denial-of-service attacks whereby a malicious node can shut out all other nodes in both known contention-based and contention-free MAC protocols [Zhang and Lee, 2000]. The ad hoc routing protocols are also vulnerable to a single malicious node because they assume trust and cooperation between nodes. A malicious node can exploit this trust by disseminating false routing information to neighboring nodes, or even worse, by routing all connections through the malicious node in order to disseminate false information.

The wireless medium also provides excellent cover for malicious users. Because wireless devices roam in and out of wireless zones, have no fixed geographic point, can go online and offline easily, have much of the capability of wired devices, have relative anonymity, the devices and their users can be difficult to trace. As a result, attacks from wireless devices will likely become the preferred *modus operandi* of attackers for launching attacks against fixed networks.

Finally, much is made of cryptographic algorithms and protocols over wireless networks. Without doubt, mobile e-commerce will require confidentiality, integrity, and authentication services provided by cryptographic protocols. To do without is foolhardy. However, to believe that these protocols provides the panacea to m-commerce security problems is dangerous. The examples given in a prior section on malicious code shows how confidential data sent over encrypted channels can be easily compromised from within.

It is important to remember that while all crypto protocols may look identical off-the-shelf, it is what is underneath the hood that matters.

It is very difficult to design a solid crypto protocol, but it is even harder to implement it robustly. Flaws in the software that implement crypto protocols often make it easy enough to break crypto algorithms without resorting to brute force attacks against ciphertext. Poor use of pseudo-random number generators (PRNGs) as well as use of flawed PRNGs commonly undermine even good crypto algorithms.

Flaws in design can also undermine the security provided by the crypto algorithms. For instance, devices that use the Wireless Application Protocol (WAP) need to use the Wireless Transport Layer Security (WTLS) to provide encrypted channels between the user and the provider. However, the WTLS does not provide end-to-end encrypted channels. Rather, the channel is encrypted between the WAP-enabled device and a WAP translation gateway. The device requests Web content from the WAP gateway, which then makes an HTTP request to the target Web site, obtains the Web content, converts and encrypts it before sending it to the WAP client. An obvious attack for an adversary is to snoop the link between the WAP gateway and the Web server for confidential information which is not encrypted.

As is often the case in crypto protocols, the use of the protocol gives the perception of stronger security than the actual implementation. In general, crypto protocols are assumed to be secure until someone finds the card that brings down the house of cards. It is very difficult to tell from looking at ciphertext how strong the crypto algorithm is. It requires analysis of the algorithm, design, and implementation to find potential problems. Often times, commercial encryption protocols are closed source and not available for peer review. As a result, crypto protocols are assumed to be secure unless proven otherwise. The upshot is that consumers feel more secure when using "secure" protocols in m-commerce, which is good for the industry. However, it also has the effect of giving a false sense of security when there are so many other weak links in the system. Strong perceived security will re-direct the resources of adversaries to other weak links as discussed in the preceding sections.

7. Servers

The third main risk area in m-commerce is in the e-commerce servers themselves. This risk is not new, however, and is pervasive in all of e-commerce [Ghosh, 1998]. The servers present ideal targets for adversaries because they are single points of failure where valuable data and services are concentrated. Most servers are vulnerable to denial-of-service (DoS) attacks as the distributed DoS attacks against the largest e-commerce sites in February, 2000 vividly illustrated [Garber, 2000].

Targeting a server makes more sense than targeting many individual clients. The return on investment is greater. Breaking into a single server has yielded over 300,000 credit card numbers of customers of an e-commerce site. If one wanted to compromise the integrity of a financial institution, what better way than to break into its Web site and simply vandalize its Web pages, let alone gain access to its customers' online accounts?

E-commerce servers also run very complex software applications such as Web servers, FTP servers, mail servers, DNS servers, and many more. Most of these services have known software flaws that if not properly patched are vulnerable to attack. Hosted e-commerce sites will often run content updating services such as Microsoft FrontPages as well as remote access administration software to allow businesses to update their online content on demand and support maintenance. These services, of course, if hacked, can give adversaries the same ability.

E-commerce sites offer more than front-end servers, however. They will usually run complex middleware programs such as CGI scripts, Java servlets, application servers, and component-based software such as Enterprise Java Beans, Java 2 Enterprise Edition (J2EE), CORBA, COM, and DCOM components. One reason for the emergence of component-based software on e-commerce sites is the complexity of the software necessary to implement business application logic. This complexity, in turn, introduces more software flaws that can be exploited for malicious gain.

In e-commerce environments, the back-end business infrastructure requires additional complexity at the middleware layer. Enterprise Resource Planning (ERP), Supply Chain Management (SCM), and Customer Relationship Management (CRM) software packages are all becoming necessary software tools to manage the complexity of end-to-end e-commerce systems [Lewis, 2000]. B2B e-commerce requires the development of middleware solutions that allow these different and often incompatible packages to talk to each other across enterprises, fomenting a market for inter-Enterprise Application Integration. The upshot, again, is that complexity in e-commerce software is making the job much harder for system administrators and integrators and easier for hackers to compromise systems. Requirements to support wireless devices in m-commerce introduces even more complexity at the middleware later for translating Web content for multiple client types, such as Wireless Markup Language (WML) data conversion for WAP-enabled clients [Lewis, 2000].

Finally, the back-end infrastructure, itself, needs to be secured. Back-end databases, legacy systems, and ERP/SCM packages need to be secured against both insider and outsider attacks. The back-end systems represent the valuable business assets of any online business. If these systems are compromised, the potential loss is catastrophic to business. Simply bolting Internet access onto the side of legacy systems is a dangerous practice. Rather, the system design must account for the new risks to legacy systems brought to untrusted networks such as the Internet. Even if these systems are placed behind firewalls, they are still linked to the untrusted Internet via the middleware layer, which is trusted. Thus, compromising these systems is not a far stretch from penetrating the front-end servers and using middleware scripts and programs to gain access to back-end systems. Strong authentication and rigorous authorization to access back-end databases from the front-end Web interface is essential.

Unfortunately, even simple flaws in the complex middleware layer can provide the leverage necessary to bypass even strong authentication schemes. Whereas most front-end and back-end systems are commercial off-the-shelf (COTS) software packages, a good portion of the middleware software is necessarily custom-developed in order to implement every business's particular application logic. The most significant weak link in server-side systems is the middleware layer. Therefore, a strong risk management plan will focus on providing rigorous software assurance for the middleware software.

8.   Summary and Conclusions

This chapter presented several new risks in mobile e-commerce systems. One of the main goals of this chapter is to dispel the notion that m-commerce systems will be secured simply by using off-the-shelf encryption protocols. Instead, this chapter highlighted weak links in several components in m-commerce systems. As in most e-commerce systems, the system is only as strong as its weakest link. Furthermore, the weakest link actually directs the efforts of adversaries for reasons of efficiency and return on investment.

While many of the risks of fixed-wire Internet-based commerce will pervade mobile e-commerce, mobile e-commerce itself presents new risks. The nature of the medium requires a degree of trust and cooperation between member nodes in networks that can be exploited by malicious entities to deny service as well as collect confidential information and disseminate false information.

Encrypted communication protocols are necessary to provide confidentiality, integrity, and authentication services for mobile e-commerce applications. However, the protocols, themselves, present their own unique risks as discussed earlier. Perhaps the greatest risk of encrypted communication links is the false sense of security they provide wireless users and purveyors of mobile e-commerce.

Probably the most significant risks for m-commerce systems are in malicious code that will begin to penetrated wireless devices and in flawed software that runs on both wireless devices as well as m-commerce servers. Malicious code has the ability to undermine other security technologies such as signing, authentication, and encryption because they run resident to the device with all the privileges of the owner. As agent-based commerce becomes an integral part of m-commerce, it will be difficult to distinguish malicious agents from benign ones. If agents are given the authority or proxy to act on behalf of the device's owner in both a commercial and legal sense, then the ramifications of malicious code attacks grow even more significantly.

Mobile e-commerce servers are particularly vulnerable to application-based attacks because of the growing complexity of the software that runs these systems. Software flaws in the middleware layer are likely to be exploited by determined adversaries and their disciples as they get published in underground lists. The servers are particularly rich targets because they represent single points of failure and the highest return on investment for an attacker's efforts.

In summary, the best strategy for securing mobile e-commerce is a risk management strategy that begins by identifying weak links. Once weak links are identified, the threat understood, and the consequences of attack quantified, effective software risk management will concentrate efforts on design and assurance activities in m-commerce software systems.

References

[Balfanz and Felten, 1999] Balfanz, D. and Felten, E. (1999). Hand held computer can be better smart cards. In *Proceedings of the Eighth USENIX Security Symposium*, pages 15–23, Berkeley, CA. USENIX Association, USENIX. Washington, D.C.

[Bergeron et al., 1999] Bergeron, J., Debbabi, M., and et al. (1999). Detection of malicious code in cots software: A short survey. In *Proceedings of the 1st Annual International Software Assurance Certification Conference*, page C1.

[Garber, 2000] Garber, L. (2000). Denial-of service attacks rip the internet. *Computer*, 33(4):12–17.

[Ghosh, 1998] Ghosh, A. (1998). *E-Commerce Security: Weak Links, Best Defenses*. John Wiley & Sons, New York, NY. ISBN 0-471-

19223-6.

[Lewis, 2000] Lewis, B. (2000). Beyond e-mail: Enterprise integration issues for mobile e-commerce. In *Proceedings of the Wireless Data Forum*. Wireless Data Forum. Austin, TX.

[Lewis, 1999] Lewis, T. (1999). Ubinet: The ubiquitous internet will be wireless. *IEEE Computer*, 32(10):128,126–127.

[Royer and Toh, 1999] Royer, E. and Toh, C. (1999). A review of current routing protocols for ad hoc mobile wireless networks. *IEEE Personal Communications*, 6(2):46–55.

[Zerega, 1999] Zerega, B. (1999). The 3g force. *Red Herring*, pages 84–88.

[Zhang and Lee, 2000] Zhang, Y. and Lee, W. (2000). Intrusion detection in wireless ad-hoc networks. In *Proceedings of the ACM/IEEE MobiCom 2000*.

Chapter 4

PROBLEMS IN POLICING E-COMMERCE CRIME

Marc D. Goodman

marc.goodman@atomictangerine.com

Scenario

Nothing works. Despite repeated attempts by FedEx employees and customers around the globe, suddenly no information is available. Everything was fine a few moments ago, but now the company, which delivers more than three million express packages to 210 countries each working day, has had its worldwide operations crippled by a failure of its information system.[1] Unbeknownst to FedEx officials, the debilitating disruption in its ability to move goods around the globe is the result of a "denial of service attack" by an unknown criminal hacker.[2]

The attack seems to have come from a computer in Germany. Tracing the hacker's steps backward revealed that he accessed a German computer via a telnet connection from a network in Russia. The Russian connection was completed via the execution of an rlogin protocol from a network dial-up access point in Brazil. The attacker gained access to the Brazilian network via a radio-modem connection in Sao Paolo.

As a result of one hacker's criminal behavior, millions of packages around the globe have come to a grinding halt. Blood and medicine cannot be delivered to patients in dire need, critical business documents and contracts do not arrive, and perishable goods sit rotting on trucks and in warehouses. Sadly, due to the legal and technical obstacles in investigating computer crime, law enforcement officials remain powerless to act.

1. Barriers to the Investigation of Computer Crime

As we enter the 21st century, national legal regimes will be of limited use to society in its efforts to control and regulate the global information infrastructure. In order to prevent an explosive growth in computer crime and cyberterrorism, there must be a harmonization of international criminal law and information technology policy. Only through cooperation in the investigation and prosecution of these transnational crimes, can malicious conduct, such as that described in the aforementioned scenario, be prevented and punished.

The challenges to law enforcement are daunting. In the conjured FedEx example, if the police wanted to pursue the digital version of a "blood trail", they would have to reconstruct data connections over a panoply of computer networks and telephone systems spanning the globe. Their first step would logically be an attempt to identify how the hacker attacked FedEx's system. Assuming that were possible, law enforcement authorities might then toil to trace back the hacker to the point of origin of his initial entry on to the communications network.

A trace of that nature would require examining the log files of each and every individual network accessed by the perpetrator. In order to do so, however, police and prosecutors in one nation would have to receive access to network data located in other sovereign nations. Of course many companies, respectful of their customers' privacy, would not be motivated to reveal the identities of their subscribers. The police could attempt to coerce the production of such evidence, but again, would most likely meet with great frustration for many of the reasons outlined below.

In some nations, connection data for local telephone calls are not kept. Were a criminal hacker to have invaded a computer network via a local modem connection, the tracing and identification process would already be severely complicated and perhaps even defeated. The same would be true had the hacker used a prepaid mobile phone, especially since many nations do not retain identification data on these type of phone sales. Police could turn to Internet Service Providers (ISP) for assistance, but technical "brick-walls" might stop them at every turn. In order to trace back an individual user, he or she would have to have been using a non-forged static Internet Protocol (IP) address. Were the ISP to use dynamic addressing, as is common practices in many regions, the IP address of the perpetrator would be lost when his connection ended and immediately reassigned to another user. Thus a search by Brazilian authorities might, if the police were lucky, only reveal the IP address of the aggressor. Unfortunately, without the information delineating which accounts were assigned to which IP addresses at which time, it would not be possible to identify the user responsible for the attack.

If by some miracle, the ISP did keep appropriate data and the user were identified, this evidence would have to be appropriately preserved and presented for trial in a criminal court in the United States (home location of FedEx's computer system). Hypothetically speaking, however, what if the data were seized by Sao Paolo police without a warrant? Would it still be admissible as evidence for trial in America? Of course the same legal question could be posed for evidence seized anywhere along the way traveled by the hacker as he looped and weaved his way across the telecommunications systems of several nations.

Of course, legal frustrations do not end there. If the hacker were identified and happened to be a Brazilian citizen, could he be forced to face trial in the United States? Perhaps not. Were the hacker to fight extradition, what recourse might the United States government have to secure his arrest and conviction within its own jurisdiction? The answer is very little. Why? Because even though a valid American arrest warrant could be issued for the suspect's arrest, if Brazil did not have a law against computer hacking on its books, it would be unable to honor the extradition request (a concept known as double or dual criminality).[3]

Thus, in the previously described scenario, the perpetrator could not be held criminally liable for his actions due to shortcomings in both international and domestic law. Despite having caused millions of dollars in damage—and perhaps even the loss of life—the criminal hacker could go free, a move likely to sour diplomatic relations between two traditionally strong allies.

In order for the United States to gain custody of the Brazilian criminal, there would have to have been a Mutual Legal Assistance Treaty (MLAT) or a specific extradition treaty with the United States allowing for the extradition of computer crime offenders. Unfortunately, most nations do not have such treaties with one another. Of course, even if such a treaty existed, completing the paperwork in this matter would prove a logistical and time-consuming nightmare. The Federal Bureau of Investigation would have to forward the case to the United States Department of Justice which would secure an arrest warrant and forward it to United States Secretary of State.

The Secretary of State would send on the request to the foreign minister of Brazil, who would pass it along to the Brazilian Ministry of Justice. Ultimately the Brazilian Minister of Justice would determine whether the suspect could be arrested and extradited. This process however, could not be completed within in a matter of minutes as was the case with the perpetration of the crime. Rather, the legal process required to secure the arrest and extradition of the responsible criminal could take years given the currently required legal and bureaucratic machinations required for such a request. Given that the world is moving more and more quickly on a standard affectionately known as Internet time, it is clear the old legal methods of dealing with transnational crime must change to remain relevant, let alone effective.

Although the legal nightmare depicted in the previous scenario may sound far-fetched, indeed it is not. Though the scope of the damage may have been exaggerated, in fact, the underlying legal questions raised are quite real. They are remarkably similar to the case of Julio Cesar Ardita, a young Argentine man who used his computer to break into the network systems of the U.S. Navy, the U.S. National Aeronautics and Space Administration (NASA), and Harvard University, among others.[4] In 1995, Ardita used his computer system to cause hundreds of thousands of dollars of damage to highly sensitive information systems of the U.S. government. Though the United States eventually identified Ardita, and secured a warrant for his arrest, he could not be extradited from Argentina due to any legal prohibitions against computer crime in Argentina. Thus the principle of dual criminality did not invoke.[5] Though the harm caused by Ardita was quite real, the law was unable to keep pace with him as he looped and weaved his way across a number of international computer networks.

2.   Why National Law Will Fail to Address the Problem

National borders are just speed bumps on the information superhighway.[6]

We have heard it a million times. The phrases are so overused that they have almost become meaningless. Notions of information revolutions, Third Waves, information superhighways, and cyber-anything have captivated the attention of journalists and politicians around most of the Western world. Yet despite their almost hackneyed connotations, societies around us are indeed changing and doing so at a rate unknown in the history of mankind. Our world is growing increasingly connected and information moves from one jurisdiction to another without any border checks in a matter of seconds. Though the virtues of these technological changes are often extolled, less consideration is given to the problems they may pose for society at-large. These changes do, however, have serious consequences that will be examined throughout this chapter.

Computer systems offer some new and highly sophisticated opportunities for law breaking. Furthermore, they create the potential to commit traditional types of crimes in non-traditional ways. Today, society relies on computerized systems for almost all social infrastructures, from air traffic control to medical service coordination to national security and defense. Even a small glitch in the operation of these highly interconnected systems can put human lives in danger. Society's dependence on computer systems, therefore, has a profound human dimension. The rapid transnational expansion of large-scale computer networks and the ability to access many systems through regular telephone lines increases the vulnerability of these systems and the opportunity for their misuse through criminal activity. Not only does computer crime have serious economic consequences, but it also carries with it the often-ignored additional costs to human peace and security.[7]

National boundaries, which in the past may have hindered the activities of criminals, are effectively disappearing with the advent of modern telecommunications systems. Thus, when gathering evidence, criminal investigators must not only be able to understand and deal with legal issues at home, but also with increasingly international issues, such as extradition and mutual legal assistance treaties. These complications are compounded as the laws of evidence, criminal procedure and data protection of other jurisdictions must be considered when pursuing international computer crime investigations.

Unfortunately, national laws, traditional policing structures, and international treaties have not kept pace with the rapid advances in computer technology. Though some nations have started to address these issues in their national penal laws, most others have not. Indeed, no one nation or regional body has come close to overcoming the myriad legal, policing, and prevention problems associated with computer crime. On the international level, these problems and shortcomings are significantly magnified. Computer crime is perhaps the fastest growing form of transnational crime and effectively addressing it requires concerted international cooperation. This can only happen, however, if there is a common framework for understanding what the problem is and what solutions there may be.[8]

It is for that reason that there needs to be a harmonization of international criminal law such that there is an effective tool with which to redress transnational computer crime and cyberterrorism. This is particularly true as traditional notions of jurisdiction become more and more outdated in a world divided not into nations, states, and provinces but networks, domains, and hosts.[9]

Given the two aforementioned ways of viewing the world, there will continue to be a natural tension between the need for the unencumbered movement of information required for the global networked economy and efforts to restrict access to data in an effort to protect proprietary information systems. As a result, society will continue to be confronted with the conflict between global networks and the national legal systems regulatory structures, and telecommunications systems that control their operation.[10] What is required is significant harmonization, reciprocity, and cooperation on the part of international law enforcement structures in an effort to make the investigation and prosecution of computer crime function and operate more smoothly across transnational boundaries. This, however, may prove to be a near impossibility given strongly nationalist legal infrastructures.

To this end, governments have remained tenacious in their national efforts to reign in and control the Internet. Yet, the global network of networks has little respect for international boundaries. Thus a coordinated legal and technical approach would be required for any serious effort to stem computer crimes committed across international computer networks. It is indeed the architecture of the Internet itself that makes it so hard to control.

Many of the Internet's rules are informal and not enforced by any centralized legal authority. The Internet system itself was originally built by the United States Defense Advanced Research Projects Agency (DARPA) to serve as a means of relaying military communications in the event of a nuclear war and explosion.[11] Central to the core of this philosophy was extreme redundancy in the network allowing any message to be carried by myriad possible routes, thus increasing its chances of arriving at its targeted location. It is this information infrastructure which makes policing online activity such a nightmare.

Once online, criminal perpetrators can effortlessly "leapfrog" from one jurisdiction to the next—a maddening frustration for police and prosecutors who, due to the constraints of their national legal structures, simply cannot compete with the more nimble movements of their malicious counterparts. As Internet pioneer John Gilmore is often quoted as saying, "the Net interprets censorship as damage and routes around it."[12] It is exactly this architecture, considered to be a feature of the Internet, which makes concepts such as censorship, control, law and jurisdiction of considerably less value in cyberspace. Unless peoples across the globe can come to a mutual understanding and agreement on permissible and prohibited conduct online, the worldwide information infrastructure will continue to be at high-risk for attack. Only by achieving a global accord can we assure that no one individual can emerge from an outlaw jurisdiction and wreak havoc in the law-abiding sections of cyberspace.

3.   Making Law Relevant

Changes in law and the passage of new legislation, at even the local level, occur very slowly. National laws can take decades to change, and in the case of international law, a glacial pace is the norm. This having been said, the law of nations and indeed international law itself must be updated to deal with the problems posed by crime and cyberterrorism. These legal changes can be broken down into two general categories: those of procedural law and those of substantive law.

Substantive law refers to laws that prohibit or require certain behavior on the part of citizens. In the realm of computer crime, substantive laws are needed in most nations around the world to make malicious acts such as hacking, insertion of computer viruses, and interception of electronic communications illegal. In many nations throughout North America and Western Europe, these laws were slowly placed on the books throughout the 1980's and early 1990's. In other parts of the world, however, such as Latin America, Africa, and the Middle East, specific penal legislation prohibiting common computer crimes remain relatively unknown.

Procedural law can be much more complicated than substantive law to effect and harmonize across borders. It takes into account issues such as rules of evidence, jurisdiction, search and seizure, extradition, compelling of witness testimony and even issues of cryptography. Yet, if any effort to resolve differences in international approaches to computer crime is going to succeed, it will have to judiciously address these issues—there is simply no choice.[13]

4.   Conflict of Laws

Historically, travel was difficult, time consuming, and expensive. Going from one's home to a foreign land was extremely rare and initiated only by the wealthy. Since people infrequently crossed borders, there were few questions that arose about the laws of one nation being in conflict with another's. Indeed, legal frameworks were designed for a world in which barriers of distance, time and political jurisdiction were the norm.[14] Yet as transnational travel became more frequent as the result of the ships, automobile, and airplane, individuals of different races and nationalities had increasing contact with one another. As we enter the new millennium, however, past cross-border contacts will pale by comparison to the new possibilities made through the advent of new technologies. Today, for example, in the world of cyberspace, digital border crossings are extremely frequent and are totally effortless.

Formerly, treaties and national boundaries had provided an adequate way of dealing with international conflicts and disagreements. However, the Internet tends to ignore national boundaries. Furthermore, previous treaties have not adequately envisioned this medium.[15] Thus, problems arise when one nation's perception of what should be legal conflicts directly or indirectly with the legal expectations of another jurisdiction.

As more and more people cross digital borders, citizens of one nation may find themselves in conflict with the laws and policies of another sovereign. These political and legal conflicts in cyberspace should be cause for serious concern as they might bring with them diplomatic tensions between nations. In an effort to avoid problems such as those described above, there should be an immediate move to begin the process of international cooperation and harmonization of criminal law vis-á-vis computer-related offenses.

5.   The Hurdles to be Overcome

Before the harmonization of criminal law can take place however, there are significant barriers to be surmounted. These impediments were addressed and enumerated by the United Nations which has devised a list of problems affecting the effective enforcement and investigation of transnational offenses against computer networks. The points raised by the U.N.'s study into this matter are presented below[16]:

- The lack of global consensus on what types of conduct should constitute a computer-related crime;

- The lack of global consensus on the legal definition of criminal conduct;

- The lack of expertise on the part of police, prosecutors and the courts in this field;

- The inadequacy of legal powers for investigation and access to computer systems, including the inapplicability of seizure powers to intangibles such as computerized data;

- The lack of harmonization between the different national procedural laws concerning the investigation of computer-related crimes;

- The transnational character of many computer crimes;

- The lack of extradition and mutual assistance treaties and of synchronized law enforcement mechanisms that would permit international cooperation, or the inability of existing treaties to take into account the dynamics and special requirements of computer-crime investigation.

Of course each of the bullet points presented above could be analyzed in great depth and could individually be the topic of an essay such as this. That having been said, throughout this essay, the focus has been on the need for harmonization in international law. Though one might have the erroneous impression that no such activity has taken place, there have been many national and regional attempts to deal with the problem of transnational computer crime.

6.   Initial Regional Responses to Computer Crime

The Organization for Economic Cooperation and Development (OECD) was the first international body to undertake a study of computer crime. In 1983, the OECD researched the potential of criminal problems associated with advances in information technology. Three years later, in 1986, the OECD released its report entitled Computer-Related Crime: Analysis of Legal Policy. This document surveyed existing laws and proposals for reform in a number of Member States and recommended a minimum list of abuses that countries should consider prohibiting and penalizing by criminal laws. The suggestion of a minimum list of criminalized computer related behavior was an important step forward in the initial steps towards harmonization of international law as the OECD suggested a bare minimum of prohibited activities that nations might agree upon. Among those computer related activities suggested for criminalization were:

- Computer fraud

- Computer forgery

- Alteration of computer programs and data

- Copyright infringement

- Interception of the communications

- Theft of trade secrets

- Unauthorized access to or use of a computer system[17]

Upon completion of the OECD report, the Council of Europe (COE) undertook its own study of computer crime and misuse. The COE's goal was to develop guidelines to assist legislators in determining what conduct should be prohibited by the criminal law and how this should be achieved. Authors of the COE report were careful to balance the natural conflict of interest between civil liberties and the need for public security and protection.

The COE's report was more sophisticated than the earlier research completed by the OECD. Not only did the COE's efforts expand the number and type of abuses to be included as deserving of the application of the criminal law, but it also addressed other areas such as privacy protection, victim's rights, and crime prevention. Furthermore, thought was given to important procedural issues such as the international search and seizure of data banks, and international cooperation in the investigation and prosecution of computer crime. It was based upon these recommendations that Recommendation R(89)9 of the Council of Europe on computer-related crime was passed suggesting guidelines for national legislatures to combat computer malfeasance.[18]

7.   The Beginnings of an International Movement

Over the past decade many organizations have built upon the seminal work in this field by the OECD and the COE. Some of these bodies include the Commonwealth Secretariat, the European Union, and the G-8 nations. Despite the very important regional efforts of each of these groups, this international problem requires an international response. To effectively combat computer crime and cyberterrorism, an international umbrella organization such as the United Nations, or one of its subsidiary entities, will be required to play a significant role in the process.

In 1990, the Eighth UN Congress on the Prevention of Crime and the Treatment of Offenders adopted a resolution calling Member States to intensify their efforts to combat computer crime by modernizing national criminal laws and procedures, improving computer security and prevention measures, and promoting the development of a comprehensive international framework of guidelines and standards for preventing, prosecuting, and punishing computer-related crime in the future.

Specifically, the Canadian representative to the conference introduced a draft resolution on computer-related crimes on behalf of 21 sponsor nations. At its 13th plenary meeting, the U.N. Congress adopted the resolution, in which it, called upon Member States to intensify their efforts to combat computer crime by considering, if necessary, the following measures[19]:

1 Modernization of national criminal laws and procedures, including measures to ensure that existing offenses and laws concerning in-

vestigative powers and admissibility of evidence in judicial proceedings adequately apply and, if necessary, make appropriate changes; In the absence of laws that adequately apply, create offenses and investigative and evidentiary procedures, where necessary, to deal with this novel and sophisticated form of criminal activity; Provide for the forfeiture or restitution of illegally acquired assets resulting from the commission of computer-related crimes;

2 Improvement of computer security and prevention measures, taking into account the problems related to the protection of privacy, the respect for human rights and fundamental freedoms and any regulatory mechanisms pertaining to computer usage;

3 Adoption of measures to sensitize the public, the judiciary and law enforcement agencies to the problem and the importance of preventing computer-related crimes;

4 Adoption of adequate training measures for judges, officials and agencies responsible for the prevention, investigation, prosecution and adjudication of economic and computer-related crimes;

5 Elaboration, in collaboration with interested organizations, of rules of ethics in the use of computers and the teaching of these rules as part of the curriculum and training in informatics;

6 Adoption of policies for the victims of computer-related crimes which are consistent with the United Nations Declaration of Basic Principles of Justice for Victims of Crime and Abuse of Power, including the restitution of illegally obtained assets, and measures to encourage victims to report such crimes to the appropriate authorities.

8.   The Need for True Global Cooperation and Legal Accord

The previously described United Nations principles on combating computer crime are important as they provide a broad overview and structure calling upon nations to consider the problems associated with criminal activity in cyberspace. It must be noted, however, this particular U.N. resolution is only one among thousands. While important in scope and content, it is short on specific actions to be taken by member states to deal with the problem. For example, there are no specific activities which are proposed for criminalization, no funding allocated to deal with the problem, and no suggested future meetings dates scheduled. Of course, this is often the case with many U.N. resolutions.

What is needed, however, is an international treaty that would call upon member nations to amend not only substantive laws vis-á-vis computer crime, but also suggest coordinated changes within procedural law itself in an effort to increase law enforcement cooperation on a global basis. Perhaps the most important law to get on the books in most nations would be a law prohibiting unauthorized access to a computer system. The reason why this particular computer offense should be a priority is that it is *de facto* a "threshold crime" for all other computer offenses. It all begins with unauthorized access—computer fraud, espionage, theft of intellectual property, and the insertion of malicious code—all come about by accessing the data, computer, or network of another person without authorization. To the extent that nations can agree upon this basic principle, a solid foundation would be laid for further steps and agreements in the harmonization of other laws prohibiting computer-related offenses.

An international instrument is necessary for harmonizing domestic computer crime laws and, most importantly, for creating better and quicker patterns of international cooperation. Such cooperation can no longer follow the traditional time-consuming legal assistance channels in the case of computer attacks because it takes only a matter of seconds for computer criminals to erase the evidence of their crimes and escape prosecution. In urgent cases, cross-border on-line investigations, such as search in foreign computer networks, are necessary, but these may violate the sovereignty of other countries. To avoid such violations, explicit authorization of the country where investigations take place is required.[20]

Although the creation of an international treaty to combat computer crime and cyberterrorism may seem like an inordinately complicated task, various countries have developed an extensive body of international law which deals with information and communication. Most of this law was in response to problems similar to those presented by the prospects of high-technology crime. For instance, Morse's discovery of the telegraph led to the creation of the International Telegraph Convention. The development of the wireless radio quickly led to the International Radio Telegraph Convention, and the launching and use of satellites for communication resulted in the Convention Relating to the Distribution of Program-Carrying Signals Transmitted by Satellite. Yet despite all of these analogous international conventions, none deals specifically with the Internet.[21]

9.   Avoiding the Creation of Safe Harbors

Although significant thought and consideration has been given to combating computer crime in developed nations, the need to ensure the integrity of computer systems is a challenge facing both developed and developing countries. It is predicted that within the next decade, it will be necessary for developing nations to experience significant technological growth in order to become economically self-sufficient and more competitive in world markets. As dependence on computer technology grows in all nations, it will be crucial to ensure that the rate of technological dependence does not outstrip the rate at which the corresponding social, legal and political frameworks are developed. It is important to plan for security and crime prevention at the same time that computer technology is being implemented.[22]

If all nations of this world do not become participating members in a global accord to cooperate in the investigation and prosecution, it is quite likely that "safe harbors" might develop in which a majority of criminals might congregate in an effort to avoid criminal sanctions. For example, for many years—and to some extent even today—many criminals hid the proceeds of their illegal activities within Swiss banks. Swiss banking secrecy, a unique set of legal and regulatory principles— allowed criminals to avoid detection and prosecution by creating a safe harbor in which to hide the proceeds of illegal activities. Though these laws have been recently tightened to avoid such possibilities, money laundering in Switzerland is far from unknown.

The same problem might develop with regards to computer crime. If some rogue nation, for example Libya, were not to participate in an international treaty or convention called for earlier in this chapter, computer criminals and cyber terrorists might be able to act aggressively towards other parties and nations and do so with impunity under Libyan law. As a non-signatory to any related treaty, Libya would in effect become a safe harbor for criminal activities. The problems caused by these non-signatory members could become overwhelming and might defeat the effectiveness of an otherwise solid convention. As an analogy, what use would an international treaty banning the use of nuclear weapons be, if many of the nations with nuclear arsenals failed to participate?

Of course there are many hurdles to be overcome in the effort to get all members of the United Nations to participate in an international convention to combat cybercrime and terrorism. Indeed, high-technology crime still remains very much a concern of developed nations. There are dozens of countries where the rule of law is significantly in question. Furthermore, nations that lack widespread access to electricity and telephones are likely to have few computers and thus in turn likely to be unconcerned about computer crime. The problem is that a nation which does not adapt its laws to prohibit cybercrime may easily become safe harbors for cyber thugs. Even today, however, law enforcement concern about computer crime seems to be very much more pressing in the developed world as these nations are the most dependent on information technology and thus have the most to lose when their sophisticated information infrastructures are threatened.

10. Conclusions

In the 21st century, the right to communicate will be the main human right.[23]

The world is changing rapidly. Advances in information technology, communications infrastructures, and high-technology have precipitated significant growth and economic progress for much of Western society. Although there have been many benefits to these technological advances, there has also been created the possibility of negative consequences as well. Computer crime and cyberterrorism pose a serious threat to our global information infrastructure. This threat is unique and given the nature and architecture of the infrastructure itself, cannot be adequately addressed by any single nation.

To effectively counter the criminal possibilities created by information technology will require significant agreement and cooperation on the part of nations around the globe. The technology will challenge traditional concepts of law, such as evidence, jurisdiction, privacy, and sovereignty in ways never before considered in legal history. An international cooperative law enforcement mechanism and response system must be created to facilitate real-time coordination among police agencies, prosecutors, telecom companies, and Internet service providers so as to prevent the unchallenged growth in crime in cyberspace. Though it is beyond the scope of this chapter to suggest how exactly this new law enforcement capability might be conceived, the crucial elements of a successful such effort have been detailed throughout this essay.

Of course, the first steps in any such effort must be the realization that computer crime poses a significant threat to the information society. Although there may be a variety of technical methods for combating computer crime, this chapter has focussed on the legal and public policy aspects required to do so. Although computer crime is increasingly being addressed in a variety of regional fora, regional efforts alone will not be sufficient to curb and prevent criminal malfeasance online. Violations of law will continue to occur and the best way to avoid disasters such as that described in the initial scenario of this chapter is to work now to ensure that there is a truly international agreement defining prohibited actions in cyberspace. Such an agreement will not come easily; nevertheless, the harmonization of international law related to computer criminality is fundamental to ensuring the success and stability of the global information infrastructure.

Notes

1. FedEx shipping data for the year 1998, from Hoovers Online Business Network at http://www.hoovers.com/co/capsule/2/0,2163,10552,00.html, accessed on November 28, 1999.

2. A denial of service attack basically deprives a computer owner and his legitimate users from accessing their own machine. It is completed through a sophisticated attack of electronic messages which bombards the victim's system with so many bogus messages that the host computer becomes overloaded and unavailable for legitimate users. To think of this crime in real world terms, sending ten pieces of junk mail to an individual you didn't like would prove an annoyance for the person receiving the mail. But deluging that individual with 200,000 pieces of mail every day would make his own mail impossible to find in the mountain of junk, would necessitate much work to get rid of the unwanted mail, and would have the effect of denying him the use of the U.S. mail service for his own purposes.

3. This "double criminality" principle is necessary to the successful operation of international criminal law. Otherwise, there would be chance of a person from one jurisdiction escaping enforcement or being held liable for an action that is not a crime in his own jurisdiction.

4. "Reno's Border Patrol Made Ineffective: Janet Reno Nabs Hacker Julio Cesar Ardita," *PC Week*, No. 14, Vol. 13; Pg. 78; ISSN: 0740-1604, April 8, 1996.

5. "First Internet Wiretap Leads to a Suspect," *The New York Times*, March 31, 1996, Section 1; Page 20; Column 4.

6. White, H. and Lauria, R. "The Impact of New Communication Technologies on International Telecommunication Law and Policy: Cyberspace and the Restructuring of the International Telecommunication Union," *California Western Law Review*, Volume 32, Number 1, Fall 1995.

7. United Nations Centre for Social Development and Humanitarian Affairs (1994), *United Nations Manual on the Prevention and Control of Computer-Related Crime, International Review of Criminal Policy*, Numbers 43-44, U.N. Doc. ST/ESA/SER.M/43-44, U.N. Sales No. E.94.IV.5.

8. Ibid.

9. Burnstein, M.R., "Conflicts on the Net: Choice of Law in Transnational Cyberspace", *Vanderbilt Journal of Transnational Law*, 29 Vand. J. Transnational L. 75.

10. Harasim, L, editor. (1993). *Global Networks: Computers and International Communication*. "Jurisdictional Quandaries for Global Networks" (Anne Wells Branscomb). MIT Press, Cambridge, Massachusetts, p. 89.

11. Ruthfield, S. (1995). "The Internet's History and Development: From Wartime Tool to the Fish-Cam," *Crossroads of the Association for Computing Machinery (ACM)*, Crossroads 2.1, September 1995. Available online: http://info.acm.org/crossroads/xrds2-1/inet-history.html. Accessed on November 18, 1999.

12. Rheingold, H. (1996). "Why Censoring Cyberspace is Dangerous and Futile," (last modified Aug. 22, 1995) Available online: http://www.well.com/user/hlr/tomorrow/tomorrowcensor.html, accessed on November 30, 1999.

13. It should be pointed out at this point in the chapter that the focus is on legal approaches to dealing with the threats posed by computer crime. Of course, in the end, the law is a good start, but other systemic problems and solutions must be addressed. The law is not the only tool that can be brought to bear on the problem of cybercrime and terrorism. Other general regulatory approaches, technical fixes, industry cooperation, and business codes of conduct can all go a long way to also help prevent the nightmare scenario first described in the beginning of this essay. Nevertheless, the exploration of these issues is beyond the scope of this chapter.

14. See Burnstein, M.R.

15. Selin, S. 1997. "Governing Cyberspace: The Need for an International Solution," *Gonzaga Law Review*, 32(365).

16. *UN Manual on Computer Crime.*

17. Ibid.

18. Ibid.

19. Ibid.

20. Council of Europe, Committee of Ministers, Recommendation No. R (96) 8 of the Committee Of Ministers To Member States On Crime Policy In Europe In A Time Of Change, (Adopted by the Committee of Ministers on 5 September 1996, at the 572nd meeting of the Ministers' Deputies).

21. See White, H. and Lavria, R.

22. *UN Manual on Computer Crime.*

23. Nelson Mandela, Address at the Telecom 95, Oct. 3, 1995, quoted in Victor Montviloff, "Some Legal and Ethical Issues of the Access to Electronic Information", *John F. Kennedy School of Government Symposium on Information, National Policies, and International Infrastructure*, Jan. 28, 1996. Available online: http://ksgwww.harvard.edu/iip/montpap.html.

References

[COE 1990] Council of Europe (1990), *Computer Related Crime: Recommendation No. R(89) 9* on "Computer-Related Crime and Final Report of the European Committee on Crime Problems", Strasbourg, (341).

[Dyson, 1997] Dyson, Esther. (1997). *Release 2.1: A Design for Living in the Digital Age.* Broadway Books, New York.

[GolSha 1994] Goldstone, D. and Shave, B., "International Dimensions of Crime in Cyberspace", *Fordham International Law Journal*, 22(June)1994.

[Joutsen, 1999] Joutsen, M. (1999), "Five Issues in European Criminal Justice: Corruption, Women in the Criminal Justice System, Criminal Policy Indicators, Community Crime Prevention and Computer Crime", *Proceedings of the European Colloquium on Crime and Criminal Policy*, Helsinki, HEUNI Publication Series, 34(267).

[NCI, 1999] National Criminal Intelligence Service of the United Kingdom (1999) "Project Trawler: Crime on the Information Highways," National Criminal Intelligence Service, October 23, 1999, Report Issued on the World Wide Web, http://www.ncis.co.uk/newpage1.htm.

[OECD, 1986] Organization for Economic Cooperation and Development (OECD),
Computer-Related Crime: Analysis of Legal Policy, Paris, August 1986, ISBN 92-64-12852-2.

[Pallock, 1996] Pallock, R. (1996) "Creating the Standards of a Global Community: Regulating Pornography on the Internet-an International Concern," *Temple International and Comparative Law Journal*, 10(Fall)467.

[Persico, 1999] Persico, B. (1999), "Under Siege: The Jurisdictional and Interagency Problems of Protecting the National Information Infrastructure," *CommLaw Conspectus*, The Catholic University of America, 7(winter)153.

[Selin, 1997] Selin, S. (1997), "Governing Cyberspace: The Need for an International Solution", *Gonzaga Law Review*, 32(365).

[Sieber, 1986] Sieber, U (1986). *The International Handbook on Computer Crime: Computer Related Economic Crime and the Infringements of Privacy*, Wiley Press, Chichester.

[SomThoBri, 1997] Soma, J., Thomas, T, and Brisette, H. (1997) "Transnational Extradition For Computer Crimes: Are New Treaties and Laws Needed?" *Harvard Journal on Legislation*, 34 (Summer), 317.

[UN, 1994] United Nations Centre for Social Development and Humanitarian Affairs (1994), *United Nations Manual on the Prevention and Control of Computer-Related Crime*, International Review of Criminal Policy, Numbers 43-44, U.N. Doc. ST/ESA/SER.M/43-44, U.N. Sales No. E.94.IV.5.

II

REASONING ABOUT SECURE AND PRIVATE E-COMMERCE

Chapter 5

STRATEGIES FOR DEVELOPING POLICIES AND REQUIREMENTS FOR SECURE AND PRIVATE ELECTRONIC COMMERCE

Annie I. Antón

Dept. of Computer Science, College of Engineering

North Carolina State University, EGRC 408, Raleigh, NC 27695-7534, USA

+1.919.515.5764

anton@csc.ncsu.edu

Julia B. Earp

Dept. of Business Management, College of Management

North Carolina State University, 2306 Nelson Hall, Raleigh, NC 27695-7229, USA

+1.919.513.1707

Julia_Earp@ncsu.edu

Abstract   While the Internet is dramatically changing the way business is conducted, security and privacy issues are of deeper concern than ever before. A primary fault in evolutionary electronic commerce systems is the failure to adequately address security and privacy issues; therefore, security and privacy policies are either developed as an afterthought to the system or not at all. One reason for this failure is the difficulty in applying traditional software requirements engineering techniques to systems in which policy is continually changing due to the need to respond to the rapid introduction of new technologies which compromise those policies. Security and privacy should be major concerns from the onset, but practitioners need new systematic mechanisms for determining and assessing security and privacy. To provide this support, we employ scenario management and goal-driven analysis strategies to facilitate the design and evolution of electronic commerce systems. Risk and impact assessment is critical for ensuring that system requirements are aligned with an enterprise's security policy and privacy policy. Consequently, we tailor our goal-based approach by including a compliance activity to ensure that all policies are reflected in the actual system requirements. Our integrated strategy thus focuses on the initial specification of security policy and privacy policy and their operationalization into system requirements. The ultimate goal of our work is to demonstrate viable solutions for supporting the early stages of the software lifecycle, specifically addressing the need for novel approaches to ensure security and privacy requirements coverage.

Keywords: Requirements engineering, Internet security and privacy policies, electronic commerce.

1.   Introduction

Organizations are hastily investing time and monetary resources in electronic commerce (eCommerce) systems to support traditional business activities. By enhancing customer responsiveness and speeding up product delivery time, electronic commerce greatly reduces administrative costs and improves efficiency. However, protecting a digital marketplace is more complex than protecting the physical one. Information is dispersed so easily through electronic transactions that it is often difficult to differentiate between illegal actions and legitimate market research or flexible actions to accommodate electronic commerce partners [ATW98, Bor96].

Concerns over the security and integrity of electronic commerce transactions initially stifled the adoption of eCommerce [Ale98, Ger97]; however, this is no longer a primary concern. Although Internet security is sometimes considered poor, it is not impeding the rapid growth of electronic commerce. Some businesses, as well as individuals, are willing to accept the risks; however, Internet users as a whole are concerned about their personal privacy and the security of their online transactions [CRA99].

When compared to information systems of the past, electronic commerce systems are more vulnerable to accidental distortion, distribution and deletion of critical transaction data [BEP00]. Transactions conveyed on paper are somewhat secure because of the inherent difficulty of accessing and searching their content, thus hindering the usefulness to abusers who might breach confidentiality. When transactions are stored and exchanged using electronic commerce systems, however, information such as credit card numbers, electronic receipts and purchase orders become more accessible. This ease of access creates the potential for wider and more systematic breaches of information privacy. Information assets are core components of electronic commerce systems; therefore, protection of these assets is not an option but a necessity if commerce is to flourish.

Successful privacy and data protection is a result of appropriate security measures. Moreover, protecting an electronic commerce system cannot be accomplished with a single security method. It is important to identify appropriate combinations of proven policies, procedures and devices to ensure the success of a secure networked environment.

Although the Internet is a promising means of facilitating the growth of electronic commerce, there remain many challenges that we seek to address. Technology problems of slow modem access and congestion are common, but are receiving widespread attention via new technologies such as ADSL (Asymmetrical Digital Subscriber Line) and intelligent routing. In contrast, software problems related to privacy and security pose a much greater challenge for researchers and software practitioners. To keep pace with the predicted explosive growth of electronic commerce, there is a great need for proven methods aimed at developing secure systems. This chapter outlines an innovative approach for designing electronic commerce systems with a direct emphasis on addressing security and privacy needs from the early stages of conceptual design.

Our integrated approach applies goal and scenario-driven requirements engineering methods for secure electronic commerce systems resulting in the specification of: privacy policies, security policies and the corresponding system requirements for these proposed or envisioned systems. Section 2 provides an overview of the state of the research and practice in security and privacy policy. Section 3 provides relevant background in requirements engineering. Our strategy (an instantiated GBRAM model for policy development) is presented in Section 4, followed by a summary and discussion of future work in Section 5.

2. Security and Privacy

This section provides an overview of the relevant work in security, security policy, privacy and privacy policy.

Security

Reducing threats to sensitive data is the focus of several studies addressing methods to provide better security for data privacy [BB95, BS96, MW98]. However, the balance between security and information accessibility necessary for normal business operation must also be considered [EP00]. Most organizations are aware of the problem of unauthorized access to personal data, but few have established an effective security program for their systems [SKR99]. Electronic commerce systems must be protected from both internal and external threats and their protection deserves special consideration during the early design stages. Despite the increased awareness of heightened security needs, most organizations are facing a shortage of security skills [Mak99], highlighting the need for a heavier focus on systems with security requirements at the conceptual design phase. Similarly, Shimeall *et al.* [SM99] highlight the increasing need for applications to be written with more concern for security to thwart the potential for vulnerabilities often exploited by attackers.

Although many organizations employ ethical codes for employees to follow; these policies provide no real guarantee against unauthorized access. The ability to determine where the business need is for security and what security features are appropriate, given the organizational environment, is vital when developing electronic commerce applications for today's businesses. The challenge lies in ensuring that the policies are reflected in the system requirements from which these electronic commerce applications will be designed.

Security Policy

The primary step in securing an electronic commerce system is developing and implementing a dynamic document called a security policy [Dea00], which identifies system aspects such as security goals and risks. It is important to establish who the authorized users might be, how they will access the system and data, how unauthorized users will be denied access, and how data will be protected within the organization as well as outside the organization.

Thoroughly planned security policies help minimize break-ins by communicating with and managing the users in an organization. Unfortunately, security policies are often treated as an after-thought [Trc00]. The strategies presented in this chapter address this occurrence in electronic commerce systems by integrating policy creation and security considerations with requirements specification activities.

Although several methods for developing specific types of security policies have been proposed [AB95, And96, ISO98, Lic97, NI94, OA95, Oln94, PFI99, SW98, Trc00], few consider the dynamic nature and innovativeness of creating policies specific to electronic commerce applications [Oli97]. A security policy must address an organization's specific risks. To understand risks, an appropriate player should perform a security audit that identifies vulnerabilities and rates both the severity of each threat and its likelihood of occurring. Today's digital economy offers more areas for risk to be introduced through the involvement of various parties, such as suppliers, distributors, customers, and partners. Researchers [Lic97, SM99] highlight the immediate need to address key research issues in current security development methods. Specific challenges to policy research raised by Lichtenstein [Lic97] include the need to address the ill-defined content and structuring of content in policy development.

The PFIRES (Policy Framework for Interpreting Risk in eCommerce Security), developed at the Purdue University CERIAS (Center for Education and Research in Information Assurance and Security), provides a framework for managing information security policy for electronic commerce applications [PFI99]. The framework addresses the need to unify security policies in a manner consistent with organizational electronic commerce objectives. Security policies must be continually reviewed and updated to respond to changes in technology as well as the business environment; the PFIRES lifecycle model supports this iterative process by managing risks as an organization adopts new technologies which may compromise its existing security and/or privacy policies. While the PFIRES plan phase does include a requirements definition step, it does not currently offer systematic prescriptive guidance to the analysts who are actually responsible for translating policy recommendations into requirements.

Trcek [Trc00] has developed an approach to security policy management that provides an integrated solution from various fields (e.g. cryptography and human management). Trcek observes that development of information systems is typically top-down, whereas security methods are incorporated bottom-up; he thus advocates addressing policy development during analysis and design. His approach begins with an analysis of the business processes and identification of individual entities to be classified into security domains. Data flow diagrams are employed to model the process in a static perspective so that information flows may then be evaluated and enforced by flow controls. Trcek identifies some important aspects of policy management, but provides no guidance for the process of defining policy requirements.

Privacy

Privacy is a concept that is not easily defined [Tav99], but it is often thought of as a moral or legal right [Cla99]. Clarke describes privacy as the "interest individuals have in sustaining personal space free from interference by other people and organizations" [Cla99]. Privacy thus affects electronic commerce consumers as well as consumers, or stakeholders, in other domains. Consider, for example, the role of a patient's information privacy in the health care industry as explored in a recent study [EP00]. The study measured privacy perceptions of employees having daily exposure to information processing activities. The findings concluded that employees are torn between their respect for personal privacy and the need, whether imposed by management or through individual thinking, to collect personal information. Similarly, there exists a need to explore these same issues within the context of developing electronic commerce applications.

Self-regulation has been proposed as means to address concerns about consumer privacy [McG99]. The FTC (Federal Trade Commission) recently issued a report to the United States Congress encouraging industry to address consumer concerns about privacy through self-regulation [FTC98]. This report was presented despite the fact that self-regulation had previously been encouraged and most online businesses still had not adopted the fundamental fair information practices that address consumer privacy. In response, [Ben99] suggests privacy seals (e.g. TRUSTe, BBBonline and WebTrust) to prevent the introduction of legislation that will be introduced if companies can not effectively achieve self-regulation. Alternatively, the P3P project (Platform for Privacy Practices Project) offers a means to enable Internet users to exercise preferences over Web site privacy practices [RC97].

Information privacy is impacted by organizational functions such as electronic commerce, database management, security techniques, telecommunications, collaborative systems and systems implementation [EP99]. Developers of electronic commerce systems need to be aware of this connection and realize the need for early privacy planning. Clearly, it is necessary to consider these factors throughout the requirements determination and software design of electronic commerce systems.

Privacy Policy

A privacy policy is defined as a comprehensive description of a Web site's practices which is located in one place on the site and may be easily accessed [FTC98]. Every organization involved in electronic commerce transactions has a responsibility to adopt and implement a policy for protecting the privacy of individually identifiable information. Organizations also need to consider other organizations with which they interact and take steps that foster the adoption and implementation of effective online privacy policies by those organizations as well. Although, organizations engaged in electronic transactions should disclose a privacy policy that is based on fair information practices, the Georgetown Internet Privacy Policy Survey [GIP99] found that Internet privacy disclosures did not always reflect fair information practices. This highlights the need for electronic commerce professionals to gain experience in developing proper privacy policies and for practitioners to have access to prescriptive guidance for specifying the corresponding system requirements. The strategies presented in Section 4 include heuristics and techniques to aid practitioners as they develop both security and privacy policies which may be operationalized into system requirements.

3. The Role of Requirements Engineering in the Design of eCommerce Systems

Requirements engineering is the principled application of proven methods and tools to describe the behavior and constraints of a proposed system. As such, it arguably influences the outcome of a software project more than any other sub-discipline within software engineering [FB91] as well as the outcome of other analysis activities such as policy formation. Lichtenstein's framework for developing Internet security policy promotes a four phase strategy to engineer information security: requirements definition, design, integration, and certification or accreditation [Lic97]. Unfortunately, the framework offers no specific methods to address the requirements definition phase. Similarly, as previously mentioned, the PFIRES framework, does not provide adequate support for translating policy recommendations into system requirements [PFI99]. Although researchers in the requirements engineering community are beginning to focus on electronic commerce applications [AP98, ACD01, Rob97] there remains a need to apply proven requirements analysis methods (a routine activity in software engineering) and demonstrate how to best apply these methods within the context of establishing policy. Goal and scenario analysis have been successfully applied within the context of evolving electronic commerce systems [AP98] as we now discuss.

Goals and Scenarios

Goals are the objectives and targets of achievement for a system. In requirements engineering, goal-driven approaches focus on why systems are constructed, expressing the rationale and justification for the proposed system. Since goals are evolutionary, they provide a common language for analysts and stakeholders. Focusing on goals, instead of specific requirements, allows analysts to communicate with stakeholders using a language based on concepts with which they are both comfortable and familiar. Furthermore, since goals are typically more stable than requirements [Ant97], they are a beneficial source for requirements derivation. Goals are operationalized and refined into requirements and point to new, previously unconsidered scenarios. Scenarios are descriptions of concrete system behaviors. They may summarize the behavior traces of an existing system. Scenarios also help in the discovery of goals [AMP94, AP98, JBC98, Pot99, RSB98]. Although the merits and benefits of scenario-based and goal-based analysis in requirements engineering are well understood, researchers are now faced with the question of how to use scenarios and goals in a complimentary fashion for evolving systems in which risk and impact assessment as well as compliance become more paramount.

Goal-Based Requirements Engineering

The Goal-Based Requirements Analysis Method (GBRAM) [Ant96, Ant97, AP98, ACD01] is a straightforward methodical approach to identifying system and enterprise goals and requirements. It is useful for identifying and refining the goals that software systems must achieve, managing trade-offs among the goals, and converting them into operational requirements. The method suggests goal identification and refinement strategies and techniques through the inclusion of a set of heuristics, guidelines and recurring question types. Four sets of heuristics are included: identification heuristics, classification heuristics, refinement heuristics, and elaboration heuristics. The heuristics are useful for identifying and analyzing specified goals and scenarios as well as for refining these goals and scenarios. The GBRAM heuristics and supporting inquiry include references to appropriate construction of scenarios and the process by which they should be discussed and analyzed. We have successfully applied this method to the analysis of systems for various organizations [AMP94, Ant96, Ant97, AP98, ACD01]. The latter two of these systems were electronic commerce applications [AP98, ACD01].

Securing sensitive data is essential from the initial design phase of a system and the cost of security controls must be appropriate for the risk environment of the individual system. A risk analysis is needed to determine the stringency of the policy. This, in turn, will affect the cost of the security controls employed to meet the requirements of the security policy. Although methods and guidelines exist for managing and developing security policies [AB95, And96, ISO98, Lic97, NI94, OA95, Oln94, PFI99, SW98, Trc00], our goal-driven approach provides structured prescriptive guidance, in the form of a set of heuristics [Ant97, AP98, Dem00], for identifying new, previously overlooked goals based on the results of risk assessment activities. These goals are, in turn, operationalized into policies and system requirements.

4.   Specification Strategies for Security Policy and Requirements

The primary goals in developing a security policy are to define organizational expectations for proper system use and define procedures to prevent, and respond to, security events. Similar to other organizational policies, the security policy must maintain and complement the organization's business objectives. The creation of a security policy for networked systems is inherently an ongoing and iterative process due to the dynamic nature of electronic commerce systems. When new technologies are adopted, an organization's security policy and privacy policy must be revisited and often times revised to respond to the policy conflicts introduced by these new technologies. Thus, there is a need for an evolutionary approach for security policy development. Our proposed strategies involve the application of proven goal- and scenario-based requirements analysis techniques in the design and implementation of electronic commerce applications. The strategies and associated heuristics are designed to ensure that system requirements are in compliance with enterprise security and privacy policy.

The steps involved in security policy development for networked systems in general, include the following activities [Sun99]:

- identifying assets centered around software, hardware, people and documentation;

- evaluating and prioritizing those assets;

- identifying risks and vulnerabilities, including the probabilities of each;

- defining a policy of acceptable use based on work ethic and culture;

- identifying necessary safeguards, including physical security, audit/logging and incident response;

- creating the plan for a phased approach to introducing the policy; and

- communicating policy to users within the organization, as well as appropriate external individuals such as partners.

When applied specifically to electronic commerce systems, the risk identification phase is more significant and critical because such a highly interconnected environment inherently sustains added vulnerabilities. A risk occurs when a threat exploits a vulnerability to cause harm to the system. Security policies provide a baseline for implementing security controls to lessen risk introduced by vulnerabilities. The number of vulnerabilities in today's electronic commerce systems is massive when compared to the earlier environments of mainframes and dumb terminals. For this reason, system developers of the present require meticulous methods for organizing risk profiles into electronic commerce systems and system policy.

The strategies described below build on the PFIRES approach for assessing risk in eCommerce systems [PFI99]. The PFIRES framework employs a lifecycle model that consists of the following phases: Assessment, Planning, Delivery and Operation. While each phase of the model is marked by specific exit criteria that must be met before proceeding to the next phase, it does include feedback loops due to the iterative nature of policy development in eCommerce systems. Risk assessment is built into the lifecycle and policy changes are classified along a "change continuum"; *tactical changes* involve short-term goal achievement whereas *strategic changes* involve long-term, broad-based initiatives. Our strategy for policy formation focuses on goals that reside along this change continuum.

In requirements engineering, "strategic goals" are those that reflect high-level enterprise goals. Since these goals are typically more stable than requirements [Ant97], they are a beneficial source for requirements derivation. Similarly, one can safely assume that strategic goals are more stable, due to their long-term nature, than tactical goals. Both strategic and tactical goals are important, but as observed in previous studies, scenario analysis aids in ensuring that tactical (low-level) goals support an organization's strategic (high-level) goals [AMP94]. During goal analysis, analysts first explore any available information sources such as existing security and privacy policies, requirements specifications and design documentation to identify both strategic and tactical goals. These goals are documented and annotated with auxiliary information including the stakeholders and responsible agents. Goals are then organized according to goal type and arranged, according to their dependency relations, in a goal hierarchy. Detailed techniques and heuristics for each of these operations are described in [Ant97]. Once the goals are identified, they are elaborated. Goal elaboration entails analyzing each goal for the purpose of documenting goal obstacles, scenarios, constraints, preconditions, postconditions, questions and rationale. Goal refinement consists of removing synonymous and redundant goals, resolving any inconsistencies that exist within the goal set [Dem00], and operationalizing the goals into a requirements specification.

Figure 5.1 portrays the activities involved when instantiating the GBRAM for policy development. The rectangles represent information sources and/or artifacts whereas the ovals represent specific activities in which an analyst engages during the goal analysis process. The figure includes the traditional GBRAM activities (identify, elaborate, refine and operationalize goals) [Ant96, Ant97, AP98], but has been tailored for defining privacy policy and security policy. As previously mentioned, a critical step in policy formation is iterative risk assessment [PFI99,

Figure 5.1. The GBRAM instantiated for Policy Formulation

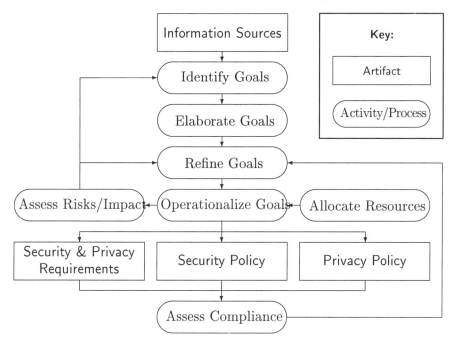

Sun99]. Risk assessment is thus introduced in this tailored version of the GBRAM; each goal is assessed for risks and potential impacts. As shown in Figure 5.1, risk identification may require one of two actions: goal refinement (e.g. by adding a constraint to mitigate the risk) or the addition of a new goal or sub-goal to respond to the risk. This is extremely important since system requirements in response to the adoption of new technologies, such as auctions [PFI99], may introduce a conflict with respect to the resulting policy. Heuristics, available in [Dem00], are applied to prevent such conflicts from being overlooked during the analysis process.

In the GBRAM, goals are categorized in one of five goal classes: user, system, communication, knowledge and quality goals [Dem00]. *User goals* are associated with the actions performed by users while interacting with a given system. *System goals* involve processing actions or ongoing provision of services by the system. *Communication goals* describe the organization and presentation of information by the system as well as general system notification and messaging [AP98]. All communication goals are functional since they involve goal achievement.

Knowledge goals are associated with information that should be known by the system or by the users. *Security goals* describe those goals involved in limiting access to authorized users [AP98]. Finally, *quality goals* describe the system, its data, or its processes in terms of standards or constraints. These categories are not mutually exclusive; that is, a particular goal can be, and often is, classified according to more than of these goal classes.

Our analyses of electronic commerce systems [AP98, ACD01] demonstrate that the availability of goal classes can be very beneficial when developing the requirements for systems since the goal classes can help ensure that all expected behaviors have been considered for the given system. When goals are operationalized, we expect a correspondence between these goal classes and specific parts of the security policy as summarized in Table 5.1.

Table 5.1. Security Policies and Corresponding Goal Classes

GBRAM Goal Classes [Dem00]	**Common Security Policies [PFI99]**
User Goals	User behavior policy
System Goals	Extranet/Internet policy Access to data policy Administration policy
Communication Goals	Administration policy
Security Goals	Password policy Remote access policy Extranet/Internet policy Incident response policy Security monitoring and audit policy Privacy policy
Knowledge Goals	User identification policy Access to data policy Incident response policy Awareness procedure policy Privacy policy
Quality Goals	Security monitoring and audit policy

The goal classes we have identified to date [Ant97, AP98, ACD01, Dem00] do not address privacy. This is perhaps due to the tendency to focus on the system perspective. However, in our most recent electronic commerce case study, we distinguished between system and user goals due to increased consideration of the users' point of view. Privacy poses

Goal	Obstacles	Scenarios
MAKE payment method selected	1. Payment method not selected 2. Payment methods not clear	1. User selects e-check as payment method 2. George isn't sure if Burdell & Assoc. has an account set up yet and needs to know to get one.

a special challenge since it is often the case that those who claim the biggest stake in a system are never really considered or involved in the design process as advocated by [BH98]. Thus, our strategy includes the participation of all representative stakeholders, including those who may not be obvious due to the nature of various systems in which privacy is critical.

We now demonstrate how scenario analysis and obstacle analysis aids analysts during goal-driven requirements engineering. Consider the following scenario for "Processing Membership Fees" from the Commerce Net web server case study [AP98]:

Actor	Action
User	find the membership application form
User	fill out membership application form
User	select e-check as payment method
User	type in public key
User	submit membership application form
Certification Authority	approve user payment
CN Server	respond to user with receipt
CN Server	increase budget balance
CN Server	create user's entry in member database
CN Server	add user to member mailing list
CN Server	add user to member web page
CN Server	send user membership kit

An event consists of an actor and an action [AAB99]. Each event in this scenario corresponds to a goal. As previously mentioned, goal and scenario analysis aides in elaborating and refining goals. For example, consider the obstacles and scenarios that correspond to the goal MAKE payment method selected, (action number 3 in the scenario above):

Obstacles #1 and 2 indicate the users' need to select from various payment options, such as check, money order, or credit card. Additional goals may be identified through the consideration of possible scenarios. For example, consider Scenario #2. George is an employee at Burdell & Associates. Before he selects a payment method, he must access his firm's CommerceNet Membership Web page to obtain the information he needs to select his firm's preferred payment method. This "walk through" approach has proven helpful in the identification of goals [AMP94, Ant96, AP98, PTA94].

Risk and impact assessment is necessary, but not sufficient for ensuring that system requirements are aligned with an enterprise's security policy and privacy policy. Consequently, an additional compliance activity is introduced. In software engineering, compliance is most commonly documented via requirements traceability [DP98, Ram98]. Traceability is a measure of quality that reduces the risk of, for example, not propagating changes across lifecycle artifacts. System documentation often remains unmodified after their initial creation and as a result often become obsolete [Ram98]. Our strategy ensures that a system's requirements specification, security policy and privacy policy are never obsolete by adopting an iterative compliance assessment activity, as shown in Figure 5.1. This final activity minimizes the risk of inconsistencies across the resulting requirements and policy artifacts by providing specific heuristics for identifying and mitigating any identified inconsistencies [Dem00]. The ultimate goal is to ensure compliance between the requirements specification and enterprise policies.

Consider an established enterprise preparing to introduce or unveil an electronic commerce system. The organization has existing policies that must be adhered to when developing the new system. The compliance assessment activity is demonstrated in Table 5.2, which follows the "House of Quality" (HoQ) [HC88] approach for documenting and analyzing large collections of requirements. The HoQ ensures that requirements reflect the enterprise policies, but requires the involvement of various stakeholders (customers, designers, marketing, etc.). The left hand column lists a set of enterprise policy statements whereas the top row lists a set of operationalized requirements, each in it's own column. The HoQ table indicates the relationships that exist among requirements and specific policies. A cooperating relationship is marked with a √ and a conflicting relationship is marked with an X. When a conflicts arises between new goals and existing policies, the goal and/or policy are refined (as shown in Figure 5.1).

In our previous electronic commerce case studies (mentioned above) [AP98, ACD01], security policy and privacy policy were not at the forefront of our analysis, as was typical with those electronic commerce systems which were introduced during the first few years of web-based commerce. It is for this reason, that we are refining and extending the Goal-Based Requirements Analysis Method (GBRAM) by developing specific heuristics to support security policy and privacy policy formation in the design of transaction-based information systems as well as additional

Table 5.2. Compliance Assessment Illustration

Policy Statements	Requirements		
	MAINTAIN member entrance to server	ENSURE content visible to members only	MAINTAIN member data history (for user customization)
Authentication is required for access to the commerce Web server.	✓	✓	
All member account information will be kept confidential and used for internal business purposes only.			X
The firewall should be configured to limit data access to authorized member users.	✓	✓	

heuristics for operationalizing these policies into software requirements. Our preliminary activity process model for this extension, shown in Figure 5.1, will be validated within the context of the North Carolina State University eCommerce Studio (http://ecommerce.ncsu.edu/studio) in which teams of graduate students design and develop eCommerce applications for industrial clients.

5. Summary and Future Work

Initially, corporate presence on the Internet was intended to provide the public with a wide range of organizational information, (*e.g.*, annual reports, product and service information [AP98]). However, the abundance of new hardware and software technologies has opened the door for organizations to also engage in electronic transactions across the Internet, raising new security and privacy concerns. For privacy initiatives to succeed, they must be accompanied by tools and procedures that provide strong security [Cra99]. Most organizations involved in electronic commerce collect and transmit sensitive information, applying internal privacy policies and security measures to ensure that this information is protected. Although there are occasional needs to disclose information, effective security measures prevent the damage that could result from unauthorized access to sensitive information, including its unauthorized destruction, modification or disclosure. Whenever sensitive information is exchanged, it should be transmitted over a secure channel and stored securely using technologies such as encryption, firewalls and access control. Data protection has regrettably subsisted as an afterthought when designing new systems; however, it is rapidly becoming a critical development concern.

Our research seeks to demonstrate the viability and benefits of applying an goal-driven approach for ensuring security and privacy by addressing these concerns iteratively and during the early stages of the software design. We are developing heuristics to aid practitioners, policy strategists and system users in identifying and forming policies so they may be operationalized into requirements. These heuristics are based on goals and scenarios that provide a common language for all stakeholder communication. The proposed strategy is one of many approaches to designing security policies, however, it provides a more integrated approach based on work in the fields of requirements engineering and information security.

The goal and scenario analysis we are applying offers a methodical and systematic approach to both formulating policy goals and guaranteeing that a system's requirements are in compliance with these policies. Knowledge of the business aspects of the system helps inform organizations about what needs to be protected. The GBRAM has proven useful for gaining knowledge of such business aspects of systems as evidenced in two previous business process re-engineering case studies [AMP94, Ant96].

The policy specification strategies and associated heuristics discussed in this chapter are being developed and refined at the time of publication. An electronic commerce systems studio is being established as a means of supporting validation of this research. Industry sponsored projects will allow us to build case studies around the process of applying goal-based approaches to electronic commerce systems. The studio will serve as a laboratory for designing such systems for industry use, while we continue to mature our strategies for managing electronic commerce policy and requirements. Studio participants will apply our strategies to various developmental situations, thus providing us with a collection of case studies to develop the necessary heuristics to validate the usefulness and efficacy of our methods. The studio projects commenced in January of 2001 with participants involved in specifying security policy, privacy policy and system requirements for new, proposed or envisioned electronic commerce systems.

Acknowledgments

The authors wish to thank Michael Rappa for partial support of this work via the NCSU College of Management electronic commerce learning center; Gene Spafford for discussions that led to the formalization of the strategies presented herein; and Thomas Alspaugh for his invaluable assistance with the production of this chapter.

References

[AAB99] T. Alspaugh, A.I. Antón, T. Barnes and B. Mott. An Integrated Scenario Management Strategy, *IEEE 4th International Symposium on Requirements Engineering (RE'99)*, University of Limerick, Ireland, pp. 142–149, 7–11 June 1999.

[AB95] M.D. Abrams and D. Bailey. Abstraction and Refinement of Layered Security Policy, *Information Security – an Integrated Collection of Essays* (Abrams, Jajodia and Podell, eds.), IEEE Computer Society Press, Los Alamitos, CA, 1995.

[ACD01] A.I. Antón, R.A. Carter, A. Dagnino, J.H. Dempster and D.F. Siege. Deriving Goals from a Use-Case Based Requirements Specification, To appear in *Requirements Engineering Journal*, Springer-Verlag, May 2001.

[Ale98] R. Alexander. Ecommerce Security: An Alternative Business Model, *Journal of Retail Banking Services*, (20)4, pp. 45–50, 1998.

[AMP94] A.I. Antón, W.M. McCracken and C. Potts. Goal Decomposition and Scenario Analysis in Business Process Reengineering, *Advanced Information System Engineering: Proceedings 6th International Conference (CAiSE '94)*, pp. 94–104, 6–10 June 1994.

[And96] R. Anderson. A Security Policy for Clinical Information Systems, *Proceedings of the 15th IEEE Symposium on Security and Privacy*, 1996.

[Ant96] A.I. Antón. Goal-Based Requirements Analysis, *Second IEEE International Conference on Requirements Engineering (ICRE '96)*, pp. 136–144, 15–18 April 1996.

[Ant97] A.I. Antón. *Goal Identification and Refinement in the Specification of Software-Based Information Systems*, Ph.D. Dissertation, Georgia Institute of Technology, Atlanta, GA, 1997.

[AP98] A.I. Antón and C. Potts. The Use of Goals to Surface Requirements for Evolving Systems, *International Conference on Software Engineering (ICSE '98)*, pp. 157–166, 19–25 April 1998.

[ATW98] R.J. Alberts, A.M. Townsend and M.E. Whitman. The Threat of Long-arm Jurisdiction to Electronic Commerce, *Communications of the ACM*, 41(12), pp. 15–20, December 1998.

[BB95] V.M. Brannigan and B.R. Beier. Patient Privacy in the Era of Medical Computer Networks: A New Paradigm for a New Technology, *Medinfo*, 8 Pt 1, pp. 640–643, 1995.

[BEP00] D. Baumer, J.B. Earp and F.C. Payton. Privacy of Medical Records: IT Implications of HIPAA, *ACM Computers and Society*, 30(4), pp.40–47, December 2000.

[Ben99] P. Benessi. TRUSTe: An Online Privacy Seal Program, *Communications of the ACM*, 42(2), pp. 56–59, February 1999.

[Bor96] N.S. Borenstein. Perils and Pitfalls of Practical Cybercommerce, *Communications of the ACM*, 39(6), pp. 36–44, June 1996.

[BS96] B. Schneier. *Applied Cryptography: Protocols, Algorithms and Source Code in C*, 2nd ed., New York: Wiley, 1996.

[Cla99] R. Clarke. Internet Privacy Concerns Confirm the Case for Intervention, *Communications of the ACM*, 42(2), pp. 60–67, February 1999.

[CRA99] L.F. Cranor, J. Reagle and M.S. Ackerman. Beyond Concern: Understanding Net Users' Attitudes About Online Privacy, *AT&T Labs-Research Technical Report TR 99.4.3*, http://www.research.att.com/ library/trs/TRs/99/99.4/99.43/report.htm, April 1999.

[Cra99] L.F. Cranor. Internet privacy, *Communications of the ACM*, 42(2), pp. 28–38, February 1999.

[Dea00] T. Dean. *Network+: Guide to Networks*, Course Technology, 2000.

[Dem00] J.H. Dempster. *Inconsistency Identification and Resolution in Goal-Driven Requirements Analysis*, M.S. Thesis, NC State University, Raleigh, NC, May 2000.

[DP98] R. Dömges and K. Pohl, Adapting Traceability Environments to Project-Specific Needs, *Communications of the ACM*, 41(12), pp. 54–62, December 1998.

[EP00] J.B. Earp and F. C. Payton. *Information Privacy Concerns Facing Health Care Organizations in the New Millennium*, NCSU Working Paper, April 2000.

[EP99] J.B. Earp and F.C. Payton. Dirty Laundry: Privacy Issues for IT Professionals, *IT Professional*, March/April 2000.

[FB91] W.J. Fabrycky and B.S. Blanchard. *Life Cycle Cost and Economic Analysis*, Prentice-Hall, 1991.

[FTC98] *Privacy Online: A Report to Congress*, Federal Trade Commission,
http://www.ftc.gov/reports/privacy3/, June 1998.

[Ger97] C. Germain. *Summary of the City University Security Survey 1997*, http://www.city.ac.uk/ eu687/security/summary.html, 1997.

[GIP99] *Georgetown Internet Privacy Policy Survey: Report to the Federal Trade Commission*. Study Director M.J. Culnan. http://www.msb.edu/
faculty/culnanm/gippshome.html, 1999.

[HC88] J.R. Hauser and D. Clausing, The House of Quality, *Harvard Business Review*, 32(5), pp. 63–73, 1988.

[ISO98] *Common Criteria for Information Technology Security Evaluation*, ver 2.0, parts 1–3. ISO/IEC 15408, Geneva, May 1998.

[JBC98] M. Jarke, X.T. Bui and J.M. Carroll. Scenario Management: An Interdisciplinary Approach, *Requirements Engineering Journal*, Springer-Verlag, 3(3–4), pp. 154–173, 1998.

[Lic97] S. Lichtenstein. Developing Internet Security Policy for Organizations, *Proceedings of the 30th Hawaii International Conference on System Sciences*, Vol. 4, p. 350–357, 1997.

[Mak99] J. Makris. Firewall Services: More Bark than Bite, *Data Communications International*, 28(3), pp.36–50, March 1999.

[McG99] H. McGraw III. Online Privacy: Self-Regulate or Be Regulated, *IT Professional*, IEEE Computer Society, 1(2), pp. 18–19, 1999.

[MW98] N. Memon and P.W. Wong. Protecting Digital Media Content, *Communications of the ACM*, 41(7), pp. 35–43, July 1999.

[NI94] Computer Security Policy, *Computer Systems Laboratory Bulletin*, 1994.

[OA95] I.M. Olson and M.D. Abrams. Information Security Policy, *Information Security – an Integrated Collection of Essays* (Abrams, Jajodia and Podell, eds.), IEEE Computer Society Press, Los Alamitos, CA, 1995.

[Oli97] R.W. Oliver. Corporate Policies for Electronic Commerce, *Proceedings of the Thirtieth Hawaii International Conference on Systems Sciences*, pp. 254–264, 1997.

[Oln94] J. Olnes. Development of Security Policies, *Computers and Security*, 13(8), 1994.

[PFI99] *Policy Framework for Interpreting Risk in eCommerce Security.* CERIAS Technical Report, Purdue University, http://www.cerias.purdue.edu/techreports/public/PFIRES.pdf, 1999.

[Pot99] C. Potts. ScenIC: A Strategy for Inquiry-Driven Requirements Determination, *Proceedings IEEE 4th International Symposium on Requirements Engineering (RE'99)*, Limerick, Ireland, 7–11 June 1999.

[Ram98] B. Ramesh. Factors Influencing Requirements Traceability Practice, *Communications of the ACM*, 41(12), pp. 37–44, December 1998.

[RC97] J. Reagle and L. F. Cranor. The Platform for Privacy Preferences, *Communications of the ACM*, 42(2), pp.48–55, February 1997.

[Rob97] W.N. Robinson. Electronic Brokering for Assisted Contracting of Software Applets, *Proceedings of the 30th Hawaii International Conference on System Sciences*, Vol. 4, pp. 449–458, 1997.

[RSB98] C. Rolland, C. Souveyet and C.B. Achour. Guiding Goal Modeling Using Scenarios, *IEEE Transactions on Software Engineering*, 24(12), pp. 1055–1071, December 1998.

[SKR99] D. Seinauer, S. Katzke and S. Radack. Basic Intrusion Protection: The First Line of Defense, *IT Professional* (IEEE Computer Society), 1(1), pp. 43–48, 1999.

[SM99] T.J. Shimeall and J.J. McDermott. Software Security in An Internet World: An Executive Summary, *IEEE Software*, 16(4), pp. 58–61, July/August 1999.

[SP00] G.P. Schneider and J.T.Perry. *Electronic Commerce*, Course Technology, 2000.

[Sun99] Sun Microsystems. *Protecting From Within: A Look at Intranet Security Policy and Management.* http://www.sun.com/software/white-papers/wp-security-intranet/.

[SW98] D.W. Straub and R.J. Welke. Coping With Systems Risk: Security Planning Models for Management Decision Making, *MIS Quarterly*, 2(4), pp. 441–469, 1998.

[Tav99] H.T. Tavini. Informational Privacy, Data Mining and the Internet, *Ethics and Information Technology*, 1(2), pp. 137–45, 1999.

[Trc00] D. Trcek. Security Policy Management for Networked Information Systems, *Proceedings of the Network Operations and Management Symposium*, pp. 817–830, 2000.

[Woo95] C.C. Wood. Writing InfoSec Policies, *Computers and Society.* Vol. 14, 1995.

Chapter 6

PROTOCOLS FOR SECURE REMOTE DATABASE ACCESS WITH APPROXIMATE MATCHING

Wenliang Du

CERIAS and

Department of Computer Sciences

Purdue University

West Lafayette, IN 47907

duw@cs.purdue.edu

Mikhail J. Atallah

CERIAS and

Department of Computer Sciences

Purdue University

West Lafayette, IN 47907

mja@cs.purdue.edu

Abstract

Suppose that Bob has a database D and that Alice wants to perform a search query q on D (e.g., "is q in D?"). Since Alice is concerned about her privacy, she does not want Bob to know the query q or the response to the query. How could this be done? There are elegant cryptographic techniques for solving this problem under various constraints (such as "Bob should know neither q nor the answer to the query" and "Alice should learn nothing about D other than the answer to the query"), while optimizing various performance criteria (e.g., amount of communication).

We consider the version of this problem where the query is of the type "is q *approximately* in D?" for a number of different notions of "approximate", some of which arise in image processing and template matching, while others are of the string-edit type that arise in biological sequence comparisons. New techniques are needed in this framework of approximate searching, because each notion of "approximate equality" introduces its own set of difficulties; using encryption is more problematic in this framework because the items that are approximately equal cease to be so after encryption or cryptographic hashing. Practical protocols for solving such problems make possible new forms of e-commerce between proprietary database owners and customers who seek to query the database, with privacy.

We first present four secure remote database access models that are used in the e-commerce, each of which has different privacy requirement. We then present our solutions for achieving privacy in each of these four models.

1. Introduction

Consider the following real-life scenario: Alice thinks that she may have some genetic disease, so she wants to investigate it further. She also knows that Bob has a database containing known DNA patterns about various diseases. After Alice gets a sample of her DNA sequence, she sends it to Bob, who will then tell Alice the diagnosis. However, if Alice is concerned about her privacy, the above process is not acceptable because it does not prevent Bob from knowing Alice's private information–both the query and the result.

This kind of situation, which is likely to arise as e-commerce develops, motivates the following general problem formulation:

> *Secure Database Access (SDA) Problem: Alice has a string q, and Bob has a database of strings $T = \{t_1, \ldots, t_N\}$; Alice wants to know whether there exists a string t_i in Bob's database that "matches" q. The "match" could be an exact match or an approximate (closest) match. The problem is how to design a protocol that accomplishes this task without revealing to Bob Alice's secret query q or the response to that query.*

Because of its practical importance and also because not much work has been done for approximate pattern matching in the SDA context, our work particularly focuses on approximate pattern matching.

The exact matching problem has been extensively considered in the literature [ChoGolKus95, ChoGil97, IshKus99, DiIshOst98, KusOst97, CacMicSta99, GerIshKus98, GerGolMal98], even though it can theoretically be solved using the general techniques of secure multi-party computation [Gol98]. The motivation for giving these specialized solutions to it is that they are more *efficient* than those that follow from the above-mentioned general techniques. This is also our motivation in considering approximate pattern matching even though it too is a special case of the general secure multi-party computation problem. Unlike exact pattern matching that produces "yes" and "no" answers, approximate pattern matching measures the difference between the two targets, and produces a *score* to indicate how different the two targets are. The metrics used to measure the difference usually are heuristic and are application-dependent. For example; in image template matching [GonWoo92, Jai89], $\sum_{i=1}^{n}(a_i - b_i)^2$ and $\sum_{i=1}^{n}|a_i - b_i|$ are often used to measure the difference between two sequences a and b. In DNA sequence matching [Gus97], *edit distance* [ApoGal97, CroRyt94] makes more sense than the above measurements; *edit distance* measures the cost of transforming one given sequence to another given sequence, and its special case, *longest common subsequence* is used to measure how similar two sequences are.

Solving approximate pattern matching problems within the SDA framework is quite a nontrivial task. Consider the $\sum_{i=1}^{n}|a_i - b_i|$ metric as an example. The known PIR (private information retrieval) techniques [ChoGolKus95, ChoGil97, IshKus99, DiIshOst98, KusOst97, CacMic-Sta99, GerIshKus98, GerGolMal98] can be used by Alice to efficiently access each individual b_i without revealing to Bob anything about which b_i (or even which b) Alice accessed (more on this later), but doing this for each individual b_i and then calculating $\sum_{i=1}^{n}|a_i - b_i|$ violates the requirement that Alice should know the total score $\sum_{i=1}^{n}|a_i - b_i|$ *without knowing anything other than that score*, i.e., without learning anything about the individual b_i values. Using a general secure multi-party computation protocol typically does not lead to an efficient solution. The goals of our research, and the results presented in this chapter, are finding efficient ways to do such approximate pattern matchings without disclosing private information.

The practical motivations of remote database access do not all point to the model we described in the above SDA formulation. For example, in some situations, Bob's database could be proprietary whereas in some others it could be public (in either case the protocol should reveal nothing to Bob about Alice's query). The "proprietary" nature of a database might make the solution more difficult because Alice should not be able to know more information than the response to her query. There is also another practical framework, within which Alice uses Bob to store a (suitably disguised) version of her private database (a form of outsourcing), and for such a framework the solutions could be quite different. Based on these variants of the problem, we have investigated four SDA models, and defined a class of SDA problems for each model according to the metrics we use for approximate pattern matching. Of course the difficulties of the problems are not the same for the different metrics, and so far we have solved a subset of those problems. A summary of our results is listed below (the results are stated more precisely in Section 4, and the models are defined in Section 3 – in the meantime see Figure 1 in that section for a summary of each model).

- For the Private Information Matching Model, we have a solution to the approximate pattern matching based on the $\sum_{i=1}^{n}(a_i - b_i)^2$ metric with $O(n * N)$ communication cost, where n is the length of each string and N is the number of strings in the database.

- For the Private Information Matching Model, We also have a solution to the approximate pattern matching based on the $\sum_{i=1}^{n}|a_i - b_i|$ metric using a Monte Carlo technique; the solution gives an estimated result, and it has $O(n * W * N)$ communication cost, where W is a parameter that affects the accuracy of the estimate.

- For the Private Information Matching Model, if we assume that the alphabet is known to the involved parties and its size is finite, we have a solution to approximate pattern matching based on general $\sum_{i=1}^{n} f(a_i, b_i)$ metrics, hence the solutions for the special cases of $\sum_{i=1}^{n}|a_i - b_i|$, $\sum_{i=1}^{n}(a_i - b_i)^2$, and $\sum_{i=1}^{n}\delta(a_i, b_i)$ (where $\delta(x, y)$ is 1 if $x = y$ and 0 otherwise). These solutions have $O(m * n * N)$ communication cost, where m is the number of the symbols in the alphabet. In many cases, m is small. For instance, m is four in DNA databases.

- For the Secure Storage Outsourcing Model, we have a practical solution to approximate pattern matching based on the $\sum_{i=1}^{n}(a_i-b_i)^2$ metric. The solution is practical because its $O(n)$ communication cost does not depend on N.

- For the Secure Storage Outsourcing and Computation Model, we also have a practical solution to approximate pattern matching based on the $\sum_{i=1}^{n}(a_i - b_i)^2$ metric. This solution is practical because of its communication cost is $O(n^2)$.

Motivation

Why do we care about the privacy of a database query? In the example used earlier in this section, if a match is found in the database, Bob immediately knows that Alice has such a disease; even worse, after receiving Alice's DNA sequence, Bob can derive much else about Alice, such as other health problems that Alice might have. If Bob is not trustworthy, Bob could disclose the information about Alice to other parties, and Alice might have difficulty getting employment, insurance, credit, etc. But even if Alice trusts Bob, and Bob has no intention of disclosing Alice's private information, Bob himself might prefer that Alice's query be kept private out of liability concerns: If Bob knows Alice's DNA information, and that information is accidentally disclosed (perhaps by a disgruntled employee of Bob's, or after a system break-in), Bob might face an expensive lawsuit from Alice. From this perspective, a trusted Bob will actually prefer not to know either Alice's query or its response.

With the growth of the Internet, more and more e-commerce transactions like the above will take place. There are already DNA pattern databases, public databases about diseases, patent databases, and in the future we may see many more commercial databases and the related database access services, such as fingerprint databases, signature databases, medical record databases, and many more. Privacy will be a major issue, and assuming the trustworthiness of the service providers, as is done today, is risky; therefore protocols that can support remote access operations while protecting the client's privacy are of growing importance.

One of the fundamental operations behind the queries described in the examples above is pattern matching. Therefore, the basic problem that we face is how to conduct pattern matching operations at the server side while the server has no knowledge of the client's actual query (or the response to it). In some database access situations, exact pattern matching is used, such as query by name, query by social security number, etc. However, in many other situations, exact pattern matching is unrealistic. For instance, in fingerprint matching, even if two fingerprints come from the same finger, they are unlikely to be exactly the same because there is some information loss in the process of deriving an electronic form (usually a complex data structure of features) from a raw fingerprint image. Similarly in voice, face, and DNA matching; in these and many other situations, exact matching is not expected and some form of approximate pattern matching is more useful.

Background Information on Secure Multi-party Computation

The above problem is a special case of the general secure multi-party computation problem [Yao82]. Generally speaking, a multi-party computation problem deals with computing any probabilistic function on any input, in a distributed network where each participant holds one of the inputs, ensuring independence of the inputs, correctness of the computation, and that no more information is revealed to a participant in the computation than can be computed from that participant's input and output [Gol97]. Other examples of such computations include: elections over the Internet, electronic bidding, joint signatures, and joint decryption. The history of the multi-party computation problem is extensive since it was introduced by Yao [Yao82] and extended by Goldreich, Micali, and Wigderson [GolMicWig87], and by many others: GoldWasser [Gol97] predicts that "the field of multi-party computations is today where public-key cryptography was ten years ago, namely an extremely powerful tool and rich theory whose real-life usage is at this time only beginning but will become in the future an integral part of our computing reality".

Goldreich states in [Gol98] that the general secure multi-party computation problem is solvable in theory. However, he also points out that using the solutions derived by these general results for special cases of multi-party computation, can be impractical; special solutions should be developed for special cases for efficiency reasons.

One of the well-known special cases of multi-party computation is the Private Information Retrieval (PIR) problem: The problem consists of a client and server. The client needs to get the ith bit of a binary sequence from the server without letting the server know the i; the server does not want the client to know the binary sequence either. A solution for this problem is not difficult; however an efficient solution, in particular a solution with small communication cost, is not easy. Studies [ChoGolKus95, ChoGil97, IshKus99, DiIshOst98, KusOst97, CacMic-Sta99, GerIshKus98, GerGolMal98] have shown that one can design a protocol to solve the PIR problem with much better communication complexity than by using the general theoretical solutions. Pattern matching is another such specific computation, and the recent progress in the PIR problem motivated us to speculate that there exist efficient solutions for this particular kind of secure multi-party computation as well.

Secure Multi-party Protocol vs. Anonymous Communication Protocol

Anonymous communication protocols [ReiRub98, SyvGolRee97] were designed to achieve somewhat related goals, so why not use them? Anonymity techniques help to hide the identity of the information sender, rather than the information being sent. For example, when people browse the web, they can use anonymous communication techniques to keep their identities secret, but the web query usually is not secret because the web server has to know the query in order to send a reply back. In situations where the identity of the information sender needs to be protected, anonymous communication protocols are appropriate. However, there are situations where anonymous communication protocols cannot replace secure multi-party computation protocols. First, certain types of information intrinsically reveal the identity of someone related to the information (e.g., social security number). Secondly, in some situations, it is the information itself that needs to be protected, not the identity of the information sender. For instance, if Alice has an invention, she has to search if such an invention is new before she files for a patent. When conducting the query, Alice may want to keep the query private (perhaps to avoid part of her idea being stolen by people who have access to her query); she does not care whether her identity is revealed. Thirdly, in certain situations, one has to be a registered member in order to use the database access service; this makes hiding a user's identity difficult because the user has to register and login first, which might already disclose her identity.

Furthermore, most of the known practical anonymous protocols, such as Crowds [ReiRub98], Onion routing [SyvGolRee97] and **anonymizer. com**, use one or several trusted third parties. In our secure multi-party computation protocols, we do not use a trusted third party; when a third party is used, we generally assume that the third party is not trusted, and should learn nothing about either Alice's query, or Bob's data, or the response to the query.

Therefore anonymity does not totally solve our problems, and cannot replace secure multi-party computation. Rather, by combining anonymity techniques with secure multi-party computation techniques, one can achieve better overall privacy more efficiently.

2.   Related Work

As Goldwasser points out in [Gol97], in the 1980's the focus of research was to show the most general result possible, yielding multi-party protocol solutions for any probabilistic function. Much of the current work is to focus on *efficient* and *non-interactive* solutions to special important problems such as joint-signatures, joint-decryption, and secure and private database access.

Among various multi-party computation problems, the Private Information Retrieval (PIR) problem has been widely studied; it is also the problem most related to what we present in this chapter (although here we use none of the elegant techniques for PIR that are found in the literature, for reasons we explained earlier in this chapter). The PIR problem consists of devising a protocol involving a user and a database server, each having a secret input. The database's secret input is called the *data string*, an N-bit string $B = b_1 b_2 \ldots b_N$. The user's secret input is an integer i between 1 and n. The protocol should enable the user to learn b_i in a communication-efficient way and at the same time hide i from the database. The trivial solution is having the database send an encryption of the entire string B to the user, with an $O(n * N)$ communication complexity. Much work has been done for reducing this communication complexity [ChoGolKus95, ChoGil97, IshKus99, DiIshOst98, KusOst97, CacMicSta99, GerIshKus98, GerGolMal98].

Chor *et al.* point out that a major drawback of all known PIR schemes is the assumption that the user knows the *physical address* of the sought item [ChoGilNao97], whereas in the current database query scenario the user typically holds a keyword and the database internally converts this keyword into a physical address. To solve this problem, Chor *et al.* propose a scheme to privately access data by keywords [ChoGilNao97]. The difference between the problem studied in Chor's paper and the problems in our chapter is that we extend the problem to cover approximate pattern matching.

Song *et al.* propose a scheme to conduct searches on encrypted data [SonWagPer00]. In that framework, Alice has a database, and she has to store the database in a server controlled by Bob; how could Alice query her database without letting Bob know the contents of the database or the query? Here we primarily focus on extending the problem to also cover approximate pattern matching.

3. Framework

3.1. Models

Remote database access has many variants. In some e-commerce models, Bob's database is private while in some other models, it is public. In the latter case, there is no requirement to keep the database secret from Alice; however, the privacy of Alice's query still needs to be preserved. In other e-commerce models, Bob hosts Alice's (encrypted/disguised) database while supporting queries from Alice and other customers, in which case Bob should know neither the database nor the queries.

From the various ways that remote database access is conducted, we distinguish four different e-commerce models, all of which require customers' privacy:

- PIM: Private Information Matching Model (Figure 6.1.a)

- PIMPD: Private Information Matching from Public Database Model (Figure 6.1.b).

- SSO: Secure Storage Outsourcing Model (Figure 6.1.c).

- SSCO: Secure Storage and Computing Outsourcing Model (Figure 6.1.d).

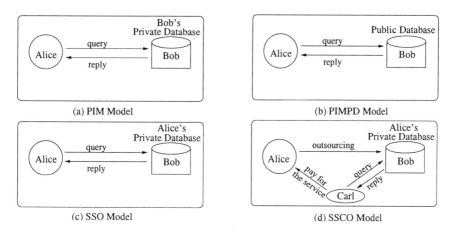

Figure 6.1. Models

For the sake of convenience, we will use $Match()$ to represent the pattern matching function, which includes both exact pattern matching and approximate pattern matching.

Private Information Matching Problem (PIM) Alice has a string x, and Bob has a database of strings $T = \{t_1, \ldots, t_N\}$; Alice wants to know the result of $Match(x, T)$. Because of the privacy concern, Alice does not want Bob to know the query x or the response to the query; Bob does not want Alice to know any string in the database except for what can be derived from the reply. Furthermore, Bob wants to make money from providing such a service, therefore Alice should not be able to conduct the querying by herself; in other words, every time Alice wants to perform such a query, she has to contact Bob, otherwise she cannot get the correct answer.

Private Information Matching from Public Database Problem (PIMPD) Bob has a database of strings $T = \{t_1, \ldots, t_N\}$, whose contents are public knowledge. Alice has a query x, and she wants to know the result of $Match(x, T)$ without disclosing to Bob either her query x or the response to it.

This problem is different from the PIM problem: in the PIM problem, Bob does not allow Alice to know any information about the database except for what can be derived from the reply. In the PIMPD problem, since the database contains only public knowledge, there is no need to prevent Bob from letting Alice know more about the contents of the database than the strict answer to her query (although Bob's doing so may result in unnecessary communication).

Secure Storage Outsourcing Problem (SSO)   Alice has a database of strings $T = \{t_1, \ldots, t_N\}$, but she does not have enough storage for the large database, so she outsources her database (suitably disguised– more on this later) to Bob, who provides enough storage for Alice. Furthermore, from time to time, Alice needs to query her database and retrieves the information that matches her query, i.e., Alice wants to know $Match(x, T)$ for her query x. As usual, Alice wants to keep the contents of both the database and the query secret from Bob.

Secure Storage and Computing Outsourcing Problem (SSCO) The SSCO problem is an extension of the SSO problem. Whereas only Alice queries her database in the SSO problem, in the SSCO model the database will also be queried by other clients of Alice. More specifically, in the SSCO model, Alice outsources her database to Bob, and she wants the database to be available to anyone who is willing to pay her for the database access service. When a client accesses the database, neither Alice nor Bob should know the contents of the query. Moreover, Alice wants to charge the clients for each query they have submitted, so the client should not be able to get the correct query result if Alice is not aware of the query's existence.

Since Bob can pretend to be a client, the solutions of the SSCO problem should be secure even if Bob can collude against Alice with any client. However, the SSO problem does not have such a concern because the only client is Alice herself.

3.2.   Notation

For each model, there is a family of problems. We will use the following notations to represents each specific problem:

- $M/$Exact: Exact Pattern Matching problem in model M.

- $M/$Approx: Approximate Pattern Matching problem in model M.

  - $M/$Approx$/f$: use $\sum_{k=1}^{n} f(a_k, b_k)$ metric to measure the distance between two strings, where f is a general function.
  - $M/$Approx$/\delta$: use $\sum_{k=1}^{n} \delta(a_k, b_k)$ metric to measure the distance between two strings, where δ is the Kronecker symbol: $\delta(x, y) = 0$ if and only if $x = y$ and 1 otherwise.
  - $M/$Approx$/$Abs: use $\sum_{k=1}^{n} |a_k - b_k|$ metric to measure the distance between two strings.
  - $M/$Approx$/$Squ: use $\sum_{k=1}^{n} (a_k - b_k)^2$ metric to measure the distance between two strings.

- M/Approx/Edit:

  * M/Approx/Edit/String: use the string editing criterion [CroRyt94] to measure the distance between two strings.
  * M/Approx/Edit/Tree: use the tree editing criterion to measure the distance between two trees.

The M/Exact problem has been studied extensively in certain model, such as PIM and SSO, but the M/Approx problem has not. Our results deal mostly with the M/Approx problem.

4. Our Results

4.1. Preliminary

Protocol for scalar (and other) products Recall that the scalar product of two vectors $\vec{x} = (x_1, ..., x_n)$ and $\vec{y} = (y_1, ..., y_n)$ is:
$\vec{x} \cdot \vec{y} = \sum_{k=1}^{n} x_k * y_k$.

We describe a protocol for Alice and Bob to compute the scalar product of Alice's vector $\vec{x}$ and Bob's vector $\vec{y}$ using an untrusted third party Ursula. Neither Alice nor Bob should learn anything about the other party's input (other than what can be derived from knowing $\vec{x} \cdot \vec{y}$), and Ursula should learn nothing about either $\vec{x}$ or $\vec{y}$. This protocol will later serve as a building block for other protocols. Essentially the same protocol also solves the asymmetric version of the problem, in which only Alice is to know $\vec{x} \cdot \vec{y}$.

1 Alice and Bob jointly generate two random numbers r and r'.

2 Alice and Bob jointly generate two random vectors $\vec{R}$, $\vec{R}'$ (of size n).

3 Alice sends $\vec{w}_1 = \vec{x} + \vec{R}$ and $s_1 = \vec{x} \cdot \vec{R}' + r$ to Ursula.

4 Bob sends $\vec{w}_2 = \vec{y} + \vec{R}'$ and $s_2 = \vec{R} \cdot (\vec{y} + \vec{R}') + r'$ to Ursula.

5 Ursula computes $v = \vec{w}_1 \cdot \vec{w}_2 - s_1 - s_2$ and gets $v = \vec{x} \cdot \vec{y} - (r + r')$; she then send the result to Alice and Bob. *Note.* In the asymmetric version of the problem (in which only Alice is to know $\vec{x} \cdot \vec{y}$) Ursula does not send anything to Bob in this step.

6 Alice and (in the symmetric version of the problem) Bob then get $\vec{x} \cdot \vec{y} = v + (r + r')$.

Note that the communication complexity of the above is linear in the size of the inputs, i.e., it is $O(n)$.

Although only the scalar product case is needed later in this chapter, it should be clear that other operations than scalar product can be carried out using suitably modified versions of the above protocol. These include matrix product, in which case Alice and Bob have matrices and R, R', r, r' are random matrices. They also include the convolution product of two vectors, in which case R, R', r, r' are random vectors. This could potentially be useful in other contexts.

4.2.   PIM/Approx

Except for the research on the general secure multi-party computation problem, this specific problem has not been studied in the literature. Unless otherwise specified, we assume the alphabet used in the following solution to be predefined and its size to be finite. This assumption is quite reasonable in many situations; for instance, DNA sequences use a fixed alphabet of four symbols. Under this assumption, we can solve the PIM/Approx/f problem. However, because the way to calculate *edit distance* cannot be represented in the form $\sum_{k=1}^{n} f(a_k, b_k)$, the PIM/Approx/Edit problem is not a special case of the PIM/Approx/f problem. We also have a solution for PIM/Approx/Edit/String problem, but because of its complexity and space limitation, we will leave the solution to an extended version of this chapter, elsewhere.

In some other situations, the above finite alphabet assumption does not apply. For instance, fingerprint, image and voice patterns use real numbers instead of characters from a known finite alphabet. The above-mentioned solution for the PIM/Approx/f problem cannot be used anymore, however by exploiting the mathematical property of $\sum_{i=1}^{n} (a_i - b_i)^2$, we have come up with a solution for the PIM/Approx/Squ problem for infinite alphabet after introducing an untrusted third party who does not know the inputs from either of the two parties and learns nothing about them (or about the query, or the answer to it). We also have a solution to the PIM/Approx/Abs problem using a Monte Carlo technique. All of these are given below.

4.2.1   PIM/Approx/Squ Protocol.   Suppose that Bob has a database $T = \{t_1, ..., t_N\}$, and assume the length of each string t_i is n; Alice wants to know the $t_i \in T$ that most closely matches a query $x = x_1...x_n$ based on the PIM/Approx/Squ metric. The requirement is that Bob should not know x or the result, and Alice should not be able to learn more information than the reply from Bob.

We propose a protocol to compute the matching score using an untrusted third party, Ursula. Our assumption here is that Ursula will not conspire with either Alice or Bob. However, the third party is not fully trusted: Ursula should not be able to deduce either x or T, or the final matching score s. This protocol works for both finite and infinite alphabet.

Let $\vec{x} = (-2x_1, ..., -2x_n, 1)$; for each $t_i = y_{i,1}...y_{i,n}$, let $\vec{z}_i = (y_{i,1}, ..., y_{i,n}, \sum_{k=1}^{n} y_{i,k}^2)$, Observe that:

$$\sum_{k=1}^{n} (x_k - y_{i,k})^2 = \vec{x} \cdot \vec{z}_i + \sum_{k=1}^{n} x_k^2.$$

Since $\sum_{k=1}^{n} x_k^2$ is a constant, we can use $\vec{x} \cdot \vec{z}_i$ instead of $\sum_{k=1}^{n} (x_k - y_{i,k})^2$ to find the closest match. After we get the closest match, Alice can calculate the actual score by adding $\sum_{k=1}^{n} x_k^2$.

Protocol

1. Alice and Bob jointly generate two random numbers r and r'.

2. For each $t_i \in T$, repeat the next five sub-steps, in which $t_i = y_{i,1}...y_{i,n}$, $\vec{x} = (-2x_1, ..., -2x_n, 1)$.

   (a) Bob constructs $\vec{z}_i = (y_{i,1}, ..., y_{i,n}, \sum_{k=1}^{n} y_{i,k}^2)$,

   (b) Alice and Bob jointly generate two random vectors $\vec{R}$, $\vec{R}'$ (of size $n + 1$).

   (c) Alice sends $\vec{w}_1 = \vec{x} + \vec{R}$ and $s_1 = \vec{x} \cdot \vec{R}' + r$ to Ursula.

   (d) Bob sends $\vec{w}_2 = \vec{z}_i + \vec{R}'$ and $s_2 = \vec{R} \cdot (\vec{z}_i + \vec{R}') + r'$ to Ursula.

   (e) Ursula computes $v_i = \vec{w}_1 \cdot \vec{w}_2 - s_1 - s_2$ and gets the resulting $v_i = \vec{x} \cdot \vec{z}_i - (r + r')$.

3. Ursula computes $score' = \min_{i=1}^{N} v_i$, and sends the resulting $score'$ to Alice.

4. Alice computes $score = score' + \sum_{k=1}^{n} x_k^2 + (r + r')$, which is the closest match between x and any $t_i \in T$.

The random vectors $\vec{R}$ and $\vec{R}'$ are used to disguise Alice's and Bob's data; the random numbers r and r' are used to disguise the query results and the intermediate results. The communication cost is $O(n * N)$.

4.2.2   PIM/Approx/Abs Protocol.   First, we will present a Monte Carlo technique for Alice and Bob to calculate $|x_k - y_k|$ (x_k is Alice's secret input and y_k is Bob's), and then use it as a building block to compute $\sum_{k=1}^{n} |x_k - y_k|$. The protocol involves an untrusted third party, Ursula, who learns nothing. The protocol works for both finite and infinite alphabets. Assume that $0 < x_k \leq U$ and $0 < y_k \leq U$ for some number U. The protocol for $|x_k - y_k|$ is as follows (where W is a parameter that affects the accuracy of the estimate, and *counter* $= 0$ initially):

1 Alice generates a random number R_k, and then generates a sequence of $W - R_k$ random i.i.d. numbers, each uniformly over $(0..U]$.

2 Alice randomly replaces half of these $W - R_k$ numbers with their negative values.

3 Alice "splices" R_k zeroes into random positions of the above sequence of $W - R_k$ numbers, resulting in a new sequence S of W numbers.

4 Alice then sends S to Bob.

5 For each number s from S, if $s = 0$, Alice sends 1 to Ursula; if $s > 0$ then Alice sends 1 to Ursula if $|s| \geq x_k$ and sends 0 otherwise; if $s < 0$ then Alice sends 0 to Ursula if $|s| \geq x_k$ and sends 1 otherwise.

6 For each number s from S, if $s = 0$, Bob sends 0 to Ursula; if $s > 0$ then Bob sends 1 to Ursula if $|s| \geq y_k$ and sends 0 otherwise; if $s < 0$ then Bob sends 0 to Ursula if $|s| \geq y_k$ and sends 1 otherwise.

7 Ursula increases *counter* by 1 if the values she receives from Alice and Bob are different.

8 Ursula computes *score* $=$ *counter* $* \frac{U}{W}$, which is an unbiased estimate of $|x_k - y_k| + R_k * \frac{U}{W}$.

Because of R_k, Ursula does not know the actual distance between x_k and y_k, and because of the negative numbers among those W random numbers, Ursula cannot figure out whether $x_k > y_k$ or $x_k < y_k$.

Now, let us see how to use the above protocol to compute $\sum_{k=1}^{n} |x_k - y_{i,k}|$, where $x = x_1...x_n$ and $t_i = y_{i,1}...y_{i,n}$:

1 Alice generates a random number R.

2 For each $t_i \in T$, suppose $t_i = y_{i,1}...y_{i,n}$ and repeat the next three sub-steps:

   (a) *counter* $= 0$.

   (b) For each $k = 1, ..., n$, Alice, Bob and Ursula use the above protocol to compute $|x_k - y_{i,k}|$. The random numbers $R_{i,1}, ..., R_{i,n}$

used in the above protocol are generated by Alice, such that $\sum_{k=1}^{n} R_{i,k} = R$.

(c) Ursula computes $score_i = counter * \frac{U}{W}$, which is an unbiased estimate of $\sum_{k=1}^{n} |x_k - y_{i,k}| + \sum_{k=1}^{n} R_{i,k} * \frac{U}{W} = \sum_{k=1}^{n} |x_k - y_{i,k}| + R * \frac{U}{W}$.

3 Ursula computes $score' = \min_{i=1}^{N} score_i$, and sends $score'$ to Alice.

4 Alice computes $score = score' - R * \frac{U}{W}$ and gets the closest match between x and any $t_i \in T$.

The communication complexity is $O(n * W * N)$. The analysis will given in an extended version of this chapter, elsewhere.

4.2.3   PIM/Approx/f protocol.   If the alphabet is predefined and its size is finite, we can solve a general problem–computing $f(x_k, y_k)$. However, we cannot directly use this protocol n times to compute $\sum_{k=1}^{n} f(x_k, y_k)$ because that would reveal each individual $f(x_k, y_k)$ result. We will present the protocol for computing $f(x_k, y_k)$ here, and then in the following sub-section, we will discuss how to use it as a building block to compute $\sum_{k=1}^{n} f(x_k, y_k)$ without revealing any individual $f(x_k, y_k)$.

Suppose Alice has an input x_k; Bob has an input y_k; Alice wants to know the result of $f(x_k, y_k)$ without revealing x_k and the result to Bob, and Bob does not want to reveal his y_k to Alice. After presenting a solution to this problem, we later use it as a building block to construct solutions to other problems.

f-function Protocol   We assume the encryption methods used below are commutative.

1 Bob computes $f(\alpha_i, y_k)$ for each $\alpha_i \in X$, where X is the finite (known) alphabet. Let m be the size of X.

2 Bob chooses a secret key k, computes $E_k(f(\alpha_i, y_k))$ for each $\alpha_i \in X$, and sends to Alice the m results.

3 Alice chooses one from $E_k(f(\alpha_i, y_k))$, $i = 1 \ldots m$, such that $\alpha_i = x_k$. This can be done because Bob sent the m encrypted results in order.

4 Alice chooses a secret key k', computes $E_{k'}(E_k(f(x_k, y_k)))$, and sends it back to Bob.

5 Because of the commutative properties of $E_{k'}$ and E_k, $E_{k'}(E_k(f(x_k, y_k)))$ is equivalent to $E_k(E_{k'}(f(x_k, y_k)))$, which could be decrypted to $E_{k'}(f(x_k, y_k))$ by Bob. Bob sends the result $E_{k'}(f(x_k, y_k))$ to Alice.

6 Alice gets $f(x_k, y_k)$ by decrypting $E_{k'}(f(x_k, y_k))$.

The technique used above is similar to the standard oblivious transfer protocol; it protects the privacy of the inputs from both parties without introducing a third-party. The communication cost is $O(m)$, where m is the size of the alphabet.

PIM/Approx/f Protocol   Now, let us see how to securely compute $\min_{i=1}^{N}(\sum_{k=1}^{n} f(x_k, y_{i,k}))$. As we discussed above, we cannot run the above f-function protocol n times to get $\sum_{k=1}^{n} f(x_k, y_{i,k})$. In the following protocol, we will use a disguise technique to hide each individual result of $f(x_k, y_{i,k})$.

For each $t_i = y_{i,1}...y_{i,n}$, and for each $k = 1, ..., n$, let $f_{i,k}(x_k, y_{i,k}) = f(x_k, y_{i,k}) + R_{i,k}$, where $R_{i,k}$ is a random number, the following protocol shows how A and B calculate $\min_{i=1}^{N} \sum_{k=1}^{n} f(x_k, y_{i,k})$,

1 Bob generates a random number R then sends R to Alice.

2 For each $t_i = y_{i,1}, ..., y_{i,n}$, repeat the next five sub-steps:

   (a) Bob constructs $f_{i,k}(x_k, y_{i,k}) = f(x_k, y_{i,k}) + R_{i,k}$ for $k = 1, ..., n$, where $R_{i,1}, ..., R_{i,n}$ are n random numbers.

   (b) Alice and Bob use the f-function protocol to compute $f_{i,k}(x_k, y_{i,k})$, for each $k = 1, ..., n$.

   (c) Alice sends $\sum_{k=1}^{n} f_{i,k}(x_k, y_{i,k})$ to Ursula.

   (d) Bob sends $\sum_{k=1}^{n} R_{i,k} - R$ to Ursula.

   (e) Ursula computes $score_i = \sum_{k=1}^{n} f_{i,k}(x_k, y_{i,k}) - (\sum_{k=1}^{n} R_{i,k} - R) = \sum_{k=1}^{n} f(x_k, y_{i,k}) + R$.

3 Ursula computes $score' = \min_{i=1}^{N} score_i$, and sends $score'$ to Alice.

4 Alice compute $score = score' - R$, thus getting the actual distance between x and the closest t_i in the database T.

Although Alice knows each individual $f_{i,k}(x_k, y_{i,k})$, she does not know the actual value of $f(x_k, y_{i,k})$ because of $R_{i,k}$. Similarly, because of R, Ursula does not know the actual score of the closest match. The communication cost of the protocol is $O(m * n * N)$, where m is the size of the alphabet, n is the length of each pattern, and N is the size of the database. In many cases, m is quite small. For instance, m is four in DNA databases.

Because $|x_k - y_k|$, $(x_k - y_k)^2$ and $\delta(x_k, y_k)$ functions are special cases of $f(x_k, y_k)$, PIM/Approx/(Abs, Squ, δ) problems can all be solved using the above protocol.

4.3.   PIMPD/Approx

The only difference between the PIM model and the PIMPD model is that, in the latter, Bob does not need to keep the database secret from Alice. Therefore, all solutions in the PIM model can be applied to the PIMPD model as well. Whether the "public" feature of the database can result in more efficient solutions is an interesting question. Although we do not yet have an answer to it, we observed the following:

Observation 4.1. *There is no secure two-party non-interactive solution for the PIMPD/Approx problem.*

Proof. A two-party non-interactive protocol means Bob, by himself, is able to find the item in the database that has minimal distance from the query.

Assume there is a two-party non-interactive protocol A which solves any of the PIMPD/Approx problems, in another words, given an encrypted/disguised form (q') of a query q, and the database T that Bob knows, Bob can find the item in the database that has minimal distance from q as follows. We use $A(T, q')$ to represent the algorithm on input T and q'.

Since Bob can use any database he wants, he can use a database like this: $T' = \{$ "axxxxxx", "bxxxxxx", ..., "zxxxxxx"$\}$, supposing that the alphabet is a set from 'a' to 'z'. After applying $A(T', q')$, Bob will get one that has the minimal distance from q. For instance, if "mxxxxxx" is the result, Bob knows that 'm' is the first character in q. Since A is a non-interactive protocol, Bob can reuse it on another database constructed for the purpose of exposing the second character in q; he can keep doing this and figure out the rest of the characters in q.

Therefore, if such a protocol existed, the query q would not be kept secret from Bob.   □

The above observation does not rule out the existence of an efficient interactive protocol or a multi-party protocol.

4.4.   SSO/Approx

In this model, Bob is a service provider who provides storage and database query services to Alice. According to Alice's privacy requirement, Bob should know nothing about the database that he stores for Alice, nor should he know the query. So Bob has to conduct a disguised database query based on the encrypted or disguised data of Alice.

The requirement that Bob should not know the query result, as in the PIM and PIMPD problem, is no longer needed in the SSO problem. The reason is that Bob does not know the contents of the database, he does not even know what the database is for, so that knowing whether Alice's query is in the database does not disclose any secret information to Bob.

Intuitively, it can look like that the SSO/Approx problem might be more difficult than the PIM/Approx problem because in the latter Bob at least knows the contents of the database whereas in the former he knows nothing about the database. But knowing the contents of the database has a disadvantage, in that Bob cannot know an intermediate result because he knows one of the inputs (the database); if he also knew an intermediate result, he might be able to figure out the other input (the query) of the computation. However, in the SSO/Approx problem, Bob knows nothing about the database, so it is safe for him to know intermediate results without exposing the secret query.

Whether Bob can know intermediate results is a critical issue for reducing the communication complexity. If he knew intermediate results to some extent, he could conduct the comparison operation to find the minimal or maximal score; otherwise, he has to turn to Alice in order to find the minimal or maximal score, which results in high communication cost in the PIM problem.

The SSO/Approx problem is similar to the secure outsourcing of scientific computations problems studied by Atallah *et al.* [AtaRic98]. The difference is that in secure outsourcing problems, the inputs are provided by Alice every time a computation is conducted at Bob's side; therefore, Alice can encrypt/disguise the inputs differently in different rounds of the computation. However, in the SSO problem, one of the inputs (the database) is encrypted/disguised only once, and this same input is used in all rounds of computations; this makes the problem more difficult.

So far, we have a solution only for SSO/Approx/Squ problem. The solution works for both infinite and finite alphabets.

4.4.1 SSO/Approx/Squ Protocol.

Suppose that Alice wants to outsource her database $T = \{t_1, ..., t_N\}$ to Bob, and wants to know if query string $x = x_1...x_n$ matches any pattern t_i in the database T.

The straightforward solution would be to let Bob send the whole database back to Alice, and let Alice conduct the query by herself.

Although this solution satisfies the privacy requirement, much better communication complexity can be achieved. Another intuitive question would be whether Bob can conduct the matching independently after Alice sends him the relevant information about the query. If the answer is true, Bob should be able to find the item t_i that has the closest match to the query x. In another words, if $t_i = y_1...y_n$ and $score_i = \sum_{k=1}^{n}(x_k - y_k)^2$, then Bob should be able to find the minimum value of $score_i$. However, because of the privacy requirement, Bob is not allowed to know the actual query x, nor is he allowed to know the content of the database, so how does he compute the distance $score_i$ between x and each of the element t_i in the database?

The idea behind our solution is based on the fact that $\vec{x} \cdot \vec{z}^T = (\vec{x}Q^{-1}) \cdot (Q\vec{z}^T)$, where Q is an invertible matrix. Alice can store $Q\vec{z}^T$ instead of $\vec{z}^T$ at Bob's site, and keeps Q secret from Bob. She will send $\vec{x}Q^{-1}$ to Bob each time she wants to send a query x; therefore Bob can compute $\vec{x} \cdot \vec{z}^T$ without even knowing $\vec{x}$ and $\vec{z}$. If we can use $\vec{x} \cdot \vec{z}^T$ to represent the $\sum_{k=1}^{n}(x_k - y_k)^2$, we can make it possible for Bob to conduct the approximate pattern matching.

For each $t_i = y_{i,1}...y_{i,n}$ in the database T, let $\vec{t_i} = (\sum_{k=1}^{n} y_{i,k}^2 + R - R_i, y_{i,1}, ..., y_{i,n}, 1, R_i)$, and let $\vec{x} = (1, -2x_1, ..., -2x_n, R_A, 1)$, where R, R_A and R_i are random numbers. We will have $\vec{x} \cdot \vec{t_i}^T = \sum_{k=1}^{n} y_{i,k}^2 - 2\sum_{k=1}^{n} x_k y_{i,k} + R + R_A$, and therefore $score_i = \sum_{k=1}^{n}(x_k - y_{i,k})^2 = \vec{x} \cdot \vec{t_i}^T + (\sum_{k=1}^{n} x_k^2 - R - R_A)$. Since $(\sum_{k=1}^{n} x_k^2 - R - R_A)$ is a constant, it does not affect the final result if we only want to find the t_i that produces the minimum $score_i$. Therefore, Bob can use $\vec{x} \cdot \vec{t_i}^T$ to compute the closest match.

Before outsourcing the database to Bob, Alice randomly chooses a secret $(n + 3) \times (n + 3)$ invertible matrix Q, and computes $\vec{z_i} = Q\vec{t_i}^T$, then sends $T' = \{\vec{z_1}, ..., \vec{z_N}\}$ to Bob.

Protocol

1 For any query string $x = x_1...x_n$, Alice generates a random number R_A, and constructs a vector $\vec{x} = (1, -2x_1, ..., -2x_n, R_A, 1)$, then sends $\vec{x}Q^{-1}$ to Bob.

2 Bob computes $score_i' = \vec{x} \cdot \vec{z_i}^T$, for $i = 1, ..., N$.

3 Bob computes $\min_{i=1}^{N} score_i'$, and gets the corresponding i.

4 Bob returns $\vec{z_i}$ to Alice.

5 Alice computes $Q^{-1}\vec{z_i}$ and gets t_i, which is the closest match of her query.

Because Alice and Bob are involved in only one round of communication, the communication cost is $O(n)$.

Notice that we have introduced random numbers R, R_A, R_i for $i = 1, ..., N$. The purpose of R is to prevent Bob from knowing the actual distance between x and the items in the database; the purpose of R_A is to prevent Bob from knowing the relationship between two different queries; the purpose of R_i is to prevent Bob from knowing the relationship among items in the database. Without R_i, two similar items in the database T would still be similar to each other in the disguised database T'; adding a different random number to each different item will make this similarity disappear.

4.5. SSCO/Approx

This model poses more challenges than the SSO model becase Bob could now collude against Alice with a client, or he can even become a client. Therefore, one of the threats would be for Bob to compromise the privacy of the database by conducting a number of queries and deriving the way the database is encrypted or disguised. A secure protocol should resist this type of active attack. We have a solution for the SSCO/Approx/Squ problem that works for both infinite and finite alphabets.

4.5.1 SSCO/Approx/Squ protocol. One of the differences between the SSCO/Approx problem and the SSO/Approx problem is who sends the query. In the SSO/Approx/Squ protocol, Alice transforms the query x to a vector $\vec{x}Q^{-1}$, and sends the vector to Bob; in the SSCO/Approx/Squ protocol, the client Carl will send the query. Because Carl does not know Q, he cannot construct $\vec{x}Q^{-1}$ by himself. If Carl could get the result of $\vec{x}Q^{-1}$ securely, namely without disclosing $\vec{x}$ to Alice and without knowing Q of course, we would have a solution. Because $Q^{-1} = (\vec{q}_1^T, ..., \vec{q}_m^T)$, computing $\vec{x}Q^{-1}$ securely is basically a task of computing $\vec{x} \cdot \vec{q}_k^T$ for $k = 1 \ldots m$, which can be solved using the same technique as that used in solving PIM/Approx/Squ problem.

Therefore, by modifying step 2 of the SSO/Approx/Squ protocol slightly, and also by using a form of "$R_\alpha * (score + R_A)$", instead of the form of "$score + R_A$" as is used in SSO/Approx/Squ protocol, we obtain a SSCO/Approx/Squ protocol as the following:

Let $T = \{t_1, ..., t_N\}$ be the database Alice wants to outsource to Bob, and assume the length of each string t_i is n. Alice generates N random numbers $R_1, ..., R_N$. For each $t_i = y_{i,1}, ..., y_{i,n}$, let $\vec{t}_i = (\sum_{k=1}^n y_{i,k}^2 + R -$

$R_i, y_{i,1}, ..., y_{i,n}, 1, 1, R_i$); let $\vec{z}_i = Q\vec{t}_i^T$, where Q is a randomly generated $(n + 4) \times (n + 4)$ matrix.

In what follows, we assume that Alice outsourced the database $T' = \{\vec{z}_1, ..., \vec{z}_N\}$ to Bob.

Protocol

1 Whenever a client Carl wants to conduct a search on query $x = x_1...x_n$, he generates a random number R_C.

2 Alice generates random numbers R_A and R_α.

3 Carl and Alice jointly compute $\vec{q} = R_\alpha \vec{x} Q^{-1}$, where $\vec{x} = (1, -2x_1, ..., -2x_n, R_C, R_A, 1)$. The computation does not reveal Alice's secret Q, R_A or R_α to Carl, nor does it reveal Carl's private query x or R_C to Alice.

4 Carl then sends the vector $\vec{q}$ to Bob.

5 Bob computes $score_i = \vec{q} \cdot \vec{z}_i^T = R_\alpha(\sum_{k=1}^n y_{i,k}^2 - 2\sum_{k=1}^n x_k y_{i,k} + R_C + R_A)$

6 Bob returns to Alice $score' = \min_{i=1}^N score_i$.

7 Alice computes $score'' = \frac{score'}{R_\alpha} - R_A = \sum_{k=1}^n y_{i,k}^2 - 2\sum_{k=1}^n x_k y_{i,k} + R_C$ and sends it to Carl.

8 Carl computes $score = score'' + \sum_{k=1}^n x_k^2 - R_C$, which is the answer he seeks.

Because of R_C, Alice cannot figure out the actual score for this query, and because of R_A and R_α, Carl cannot figure out the actual score between his query and other items in the database (except for the matched one), even if Carl could collude with Bob. The communication cost of the protocol is $O(n^2)$, most of which is contributed by the computation of $R_\alpha \vec{x} Q^{-1}$ in step 3.

5. Conclusion and Future Work

We have developed four models for secure remote database access, and presented a class of problems and solutions for these models. For some problems, such as SSO/Approx/Squ and SSCO/Approx/Squ problems, our solutions are practical, and they only need $O(n)$ and $O(n^2)$ communication cost, respectively; while for PIM/Approx and PIMPD/Approx problems, our results are still at the theoretical stage because of their high communication cost. Improving the communication cost for those solutions is one avenue for future work: We suspect that, whenever there is a dependence on N, that dependence could be made sub-linear (perhaps logarithmic) by combining our methods with the known powerful higher dimensional indexing techniques [Sam99, AgrFal93, Ary95, Kle97, BecKriSch90, Gut84]. However, combining those schemes with our protocols will not be a trivial task, and the increase in the constant factors hiding behind the "big-oh" notation may well negate the benefits of the asymptotic sub-linearity in N; for example, in a tree search for processing the query, Bob has to be prevented from knowing what nodes of his tree are visited when processing the query (otherwise he gets information about the query), which requires using a PIR-like protocol at each node down the tree. But even that is not enough: Alice herself must be prevented from learning anything about Bob's data other than the answer to her query, but in most of the tree-based schemes in the literature the comparison at a node of the search tree gives information about the data that is associated with that node (these schemes were designed for an environment where the searcher is the owner, and may require substantial modification before they are used in our context).

Another avenue for future work is the pattern matching of branching structures: the pattern matching problems that we have discussed only involve patterns of simple linear structure; in many applications, patterns have a branching structure, such as a tree or a DAG. The M/Approx/Edit/Tree problem in our model is one of the examples. Developing a secure protocol to deal with this type of query is a challenging problem.

Finally, avoiding the use of a third party in the protocols that use such an Ursula is an interesting problem.

Acknowledgment

Portions of this work were supported by Grant EIA-9903545 from the National Science Foundation, and by sponsors of the Center for Education and Research in Information Assurance and Security.

References

[AgrFal93] R. Agrawal, C. Faloutsos and A. Swami. Efficient similarity search in sequence databases. In *Proceeding of the Fourth Int'l Conference on Foundations of Data Organization and Algorithms*, October 1993. Also in Lecture Notes in Computer Science 730, Springer Verlag, 1993, 69–84.

[ApoGal97] A. Apostolico and Z. Galil, editors. *Pattern Matching Algorithms*. Oxford University Press, 1997.

[Ary95] S. Arya. Ph.d thesis: Nearest neighbor searching and applications. Technical Report CS-TR-3490, University of Maryland at College Park, June 1995.

[AtaRic98] M. Atallah and J. Rice. Secure outsourcing of scientific computations. Technical Report COAST TR 98-15, Department of Computer Science, Purdue University, 1998.

[BecKriSch90] N. Beckmann, H-P. Kriegel, R. Schneider, B. Seeger. The r*-tree: An efficient and robust access method for points and rectangles. In *ACM SIGMOD Workshop on Data Mining and Knowledge Discovery*, pages 322–331, Atlantic City, NJ, 1990.

[CacMicSta99] C. Cachin, S. Micali and M. Stadler. Computationally private information retrieval with polylogarithmic communication. *Advances in Cryptology: EUROCRYPT '99, Lecture Notes in Computer Science*, 1592:402–414, 1999.

[ChoGilNao97] B. Chor, N. Gilboa and M. Naor. Private information retrieval by keywords. Technical Report TR CS0917, Department of Computer Science, Technion, 1997.

[ChoGil97] B. Chor and N. Gilboa. Computationally private information retrieval (extended abstract). In *Proceedings of the twenty-ninth annual ACM symposium on Theory of computing*, El Paso, TX USA, May 4-6 1997.

[ChoGolKus95] B. Chor, O. Goldreich, E. Kushilevitz and M. Sudan. Private information retrieval. In *Proceedings of IEEE Symposium on Foundations of Computer Science*, Milwaukee, WI USA, October 23-25 1995.

[CroRyt94] M. Crochemore and W. Rytter. *Text Algorithms*. Oxford University Press, 1994.

[DiIshOst98] G. Di-Crescenzo, Y. Ishai and R. Ostrovsky. Universal service-providers for database private information retrieval. In *Proceedings of the 17th Annual ACM Symposium on Principles of Distributed Computing*, September 21 1998.

[GerGolMal98] Y. Gertner, S. Goldwasser and T. Malkin. A random server model for private information retrieval. In *2nd International Workshop on Randomization and Approximation Techniques in Computer Science (RANDOM '98)*, 1998.

[GerIshKus98] Y. Gertner, Y. Ishai, E. Kushilevitz and T. Malkin. Protecting data privacy in private information retrieval schemes. In *Proceedings of the thirtieth annual ACM symposium on Theory of computing*, Dallas, TX USA, May 24-26 1998.

[Gol98] O. Goldreich. Secure multi-party computation (working draft). Available from http://www.wisdom.weizmann.ac.il/home/oded/public_html/foc.html, 1998.

[Gol97] S. Goldwasser. Multi-party computations: Past and present. In *Proceedings of the sixteenth annual ACM symposium on Principles of distributed computing*, Santa Barbara, CA USA, August 21-24 1997.

[GolMicWig87] O. Goldreich, S. Micali and A. Wigderson. How to play any mental game. In *Proceedings of the 19th annual ACM symposium on Theory of computing*, pages 218–229, 1987.

[GonWoo92] R. Gonzalezi and R. Woods. *Digital Image Processing.* Addison-Wesley, Reading, MA, 1992.

[Gus97] D. Gusfield. *Algorithms on Strings, Trees, and Sequences: Computer Science and Comutational Biology.* Cambridge University Press, 1997.

[Gut84] A. Guttman. R-trees: a dynamic index structure for spatial searching. In *ACM SIGMOD Workshop on Data Mining and Knowledge Discovery*, pages 163–174, Boston, MA, 1984.

[IshKus99] Y. Ishai and E. Kushilevitz. Improved upper bounds on information-theoretic private information retrieval (extended abstract). In *Proceedings of the thirty-first annual ACM symposium on Theory of computing*, Atlanta, GA USA, May 1-4 1999.

[Jai89] A. Jain. *Fundamentals of Digital Image Processing.* Prentice Hall, Englewood Cliffs, NJ, 1989.

[Kle97] J. Kleinberg. Two algorithms for nearest-neighbor search in high dimensions. In *Proceedings of the 29th ACM Symposium on Theory of Computing*, 1997.

[KusOst97] E. Kushilevitz and R. Ostrovsky. Replication is not needed: Single database, computationally-private information retrieval. In *Proceedings of the 38th annual IEEE computer society conference on Foundation of Computer Science*, Miami Beach, Florida USA, October 20-22 1997.

[ReiRub98] M. K. Reiter and A. D. Rubin. Crowds: anonymity for web transaction. *ACM Transactions on Information and System Security*, 1(1):Pages 66–92, 1998.

[Sam99] Hanan Samet. Multidimensional data structures. In Mikhail J. Atallah, editor, *Algorithms and Theory of Computation Handbook*, chapter 18. CRC Press, 1999.

[SonWagPer00] D. Song, D. Wagner and A. Perrig. Practical techniques for searches on encrypted data. In *Proceedings of 2000 IEEE Sympo-

sium on Security and Privacy, Oakland, California, USA, May 14-17 2000.

[SyvGolRee97] P. F. Syverson, D. M. Goldschlag and M. G. Reed. Anonymous connections and onion routing. In *Proceedings of 1997 IEEE Symposium on Security and Privacy*, Oakland, California, USA, May 5-7 1997.

[Yao82] A. Yao. Protocols for secure computations. In *Proceedings of the 23rd Annual IEEE Symposium on Foundations of Computer Science*, 1982.

Chapter 7

A NEW APPROACH TO REASONING ABOUT ACCOUNTABILITY IN CRYPTOGRAPHIC PROTOCOLS FOR E-COMMERCE

Hongxue Wang

Athabasca University

1 University Av, Athabasca, AB T9S 3A3, Canada

harrisw@athabascau.ca

Vijay Varadharajan

University of Western Sydney Nepean

P.O.Box 10, Kingswood, NSW 2747, Australia

vijay@cit.nepean.uws.edu.au

Yan Zhang

University of Western Sydney Nepean

P.O.Box 10, Kingswood, NSW 2747, Australia

yan@cit.nepean.uws.edu.au

Abstract   This chapter presents a generic belief logic and demonstrates how it can be used to reason about accountability in cryptographic protocols for electronic commerce. First, we explain why the analysis of accountability properties can be treated in terms of belief. Different from other logics that have been proposed earlier to deal with accountability, our logic uses more general logical terms to deal with accountability, instead of the specific predicate "canprove". We argue that the essence of accountability is actually the ability to "make" someone "believe" something, and the notion of "make" is just another modal operator in a generic belief logic. We then describe our belief logic and present an axiomatization system for analyzing cryptographic protocols for e-commerce. Finally, we illustrate with two examples how our logic can be used for our intended purpose.

Introduction

With the dramatic growth in information technology and the increasing use of the Internet for electronic commerce transactions, security technology is occupying the centre stage of discussion and debate, because in this environment, transactions are often conducted between untrusted or even "unknown" parties via communications over insecure networks. As such, the need for sound cryptographic protocols is essential, especially for secure electronic payments and commerce.

In cryptographic protocols for e-commerce, there is a clear need for parties involved to be able to prove their claims, both between themselves as well as to trusted third parties. These are often related to resolution of disputes that can arise in a commercial transaction where it is necessary to be able to prove certain statements to a third party, such as a court of law. Such requirements are sometimes referred to as accountability requirements. Although over the past decade many belief-based logics [AT91, S90, BAN89, GNY90] have been developed for the analysis of cryptographic protocols, only few of these logics (such as [K95, B97, KN98]) can be used to analyze the accountability requirements for some e-commerce protocols. One common feature amongst these accountability-aware logics is the use of a special predicate called "canprove" and several postulates associated with the predicate.

In this chapter, we explore further the issue of accountability, and find that the essence of accountability is actually the ability to "make" someone "believe" something. We are further convinced that "make" is just another modal operator similar to "believe", because it is needed as a primitive in constructing many logical statements in many application domains, such as "a formula is made true" or "someone has made a formula true", or "someone is made to believe that a formula is true", or "someone is made to know that a formula is true". Especially, it is useful in constructing assertions on actions and results of actions such as those considered in situation calculus where "make" is represented as "result-of". Indeed, "that something is true as a result of taking a certain action" can be interpreted as "something is made true by completing a certain action".

Therefore, once we have "make" as a modal operator in belief logic, denoted by symbol $\mathcal{M}$, the accountability of an agent or a principal P for a statement $\phi(D)$ regarding another principal D can be general stated as follows:

Definition 1. *Accountability of a principal P (prosecutor) for a statement $\phi(D)$ regarding a principal D (defender) is the ability of P to make a third party A (arbiter) believe that $\phi(D)$ is true.*

and the statement "P makes A believe $\phi(D)$ is true" can be formalized as $\mathcal{M}_P \mathcal{B}_A \phi(D)$ in the extended belief logic. More importantly, the accountability for the statement $\phi(D)$ can then be analysed directly by proving whether the formula $\mathcal{M}_P \mathcal{B}_A \phi(D)$ is a theorem of the logic or not.

For example, consider a session of Internet shopping where the merchant has completed a transaction with a customer that involved the sale of a computer at a certain price. However, on the invoice issued to the customer by the merchant, the price is higher than that previously agreed. If this dispute is to go to a court, then the customer becomes the prosecutor P, the merchant becomes the defender D and the court judge is the arbiter A. On this occasion, the statement $\phi(D)$ is that "D has agreed to sell the computer at the price OfferedPrice specified online". The accountability of the OfferedPrice can be analysed by checking whether P has enough evidence to make A believe $\phi(D)$, that is, whether "P makes A believe $\phi(D)$ is true" is a theorem or not.

Compared with other definitions of accountability such as those given in [K95], ours is more generic and is not limited to the association of a unique principal with an object or action. More importantly, as "to make someone believe something" has become just an ordinary formula, proving accountability becomes the usual task of theorem proving in our logic.

The rest of the chapter is organized as follows. In the next section, we describe the syntax of our belief logic and propose few extensions to the basic belief logic. We introduce an axiomatization system in Section 2. We then apply our logic to two e-commerce protocols and reason about their accountability properties using the logic. Finally, we conclude the chapter with a summary of main contributions and indicate other possible uses of the proposed logic.

1. The Syntax of the Logic

Our logic, called $\mathcal{L}^{ec}$ hereafter, is a many-sorted belief logic. In order to formalize various aspects of knowledge in the domain of computer security, we introduce some extensions to the basic belief logic.

We first introduce the notion of domain into our logic in order to indicate explicitly what objects can be referred to by variables. Intuitively, a domain is a set of objects and hence we allow some set operations on domains. We use notation $x : dx$ to attach domain dx to variable x, use

$dx + dy$ to denote a domain that contains objects in either dx or dy, $dx * dy$ to denote a domain containing objects in both dx and dy, and use $dx - dy$ to refer to a domain that contains objects in dx but not dy. We use $o \in dx$ to represent the fact that an object o is in domain dx. In particular, we reserve *Agent* as a domain name referring to the set of agents (principals).

Following the introduction of domain, we now can make quantifiers more precise in our logic. We represent universal quantifier as $(* \ x : dx)$, and existential quantifier as $(! \ x : dx)$. Our universal quantifier $(* \ x : dx)$ is intended to imply that "for all objects in domain dx", whereas existential quantifier $(! \ x : dx)$ is intended to imply that "there is at least one object in domain dx".

As suggested by our discussion in Section 7, we use two modal operators $\mathcal{B}$ and $\mathcal{M}$ to capture the modalities "believe" and "make" respectively. As usual in modal logic, to represent notions such as "who believes" or "who makes", appropriate agent names can be attached to the above modal operators as subscripts. Therefore, by $\mathcal{B}_\alpha \phi$ we mean that an agent α believes ϕ is true, and by $\mathcal{M}_\alpha \phi$ we mean that an agent α makes ϕ true.

Now following the usual tradition [CH73], we can formally define by induction $\mathcal{L}^{ec}$ formulae as follows:

Definition 2. ($\mathcal{L}^{ec}$ formulae)

1 *(Atomic formulae)* $\phi(\pi_1, \pi_2, \ldots, \pi_n)$ *is an atomic formula in logic* $\mathcal{L}^{ec}$, *if* ϕ *is an n-ary relation constant, and* π_1, π_2, ..., π_n *are terms.*

2 *(Negation, Quantification and Modality) If* ϕ *is a* $\mathcal{L}^{ec}$ *formula,* $\neg$ *is the negation connective,* Θ *is a quantifier, and* χ *is a modal operator, then* $\chi\phi$, $\neg\phi$ *and* $\Theta\phi$ *are formulae in logic* $\mathcal{L}^{ec}$.

3 *(Composition) If* ψ *and* ϕ *are* $\mathcal{L}^{ec}$ *formulae, then* $\psi \wedge \phi$, $\psi \vee \phi$, $\psi \rightarrow \phi$ *and* $\psi \leftrightarrow \phi$ *are also* $\mathcal{L}^{ec}$ *formulae, where* $\wedge, \vee, \rightarrow$ *and* $\leftrightarrow$ *are logical connectives.*

4 *Nothing else is a* $\mathcal{L}^{ec}$ *formula.* ∎

According to the above definition, the following are some examples of $\mathcal{L}^{ec}$ formulae:

- $\mathcal{B}_{Flash}isFireWall(Karak)$.
  It states that agent *Flash* believes that *Karak* is a firewall machine.

- $\mathcal{M}_{Andrew}(available(Karak))$.
  It says that agent Andrew makes computer Karak available.

- $((*cx : Client)(*mx : KeyReq)receive(KDC, mx, cx))$
  $\rightarrow (!\, ax : KDC)\mathcal{M}_{ax}produce(mx, kx) \wedge send(KDC, kx, cx)$.
  It says that, if the key distribution centre received a key request
  from a client within the organization, there should be an agent to
  produce the required key and send the key back to the client.

Obviously, the above constructs are still very generic, and can be used
to formalize many different aspects of the world. In the following, we
shall introduce objects, domains and predicates that are specific to the
analysis of cryptographic protocols.

Specific Domains, Objects and Functions

In addition to *Agent*, we also identify *Key*, *KeyReq*, *Nonce*, *Message*,
Certificate and *TimeStamp* as relevant domains in the context of cryptographic protocol analysis. In this chapter, we use K^+ to denote public
keys, K^- to denote private keys. In general, we use K to denote keys
or secret keys. In particular, we use K_α^+ and K_α^- to denote an agent
α's public and private keys respectively, and use K_{bc} or K_{cb} to denote a
shared key between two agents b and c. We use N to denote nonces, N_α
to denote a nonce generated by agent α. Similarly, we use T to denote
timestamps, and T_α to denote a timestamp generated by α. We use CT
to denote a certificate, and CT_α to denote a certificate of agent α. We
use X with or without a subscript to denote objects in general, and use
$h(X)$ to represent a hash value from X.

Messages are important elements of any protocol. A message is either
primitive or composite. Primitive messages include public, private or
shared keys, nonces, names of agents, numerical constants, and even
logical formulas; whereas a composite message is made up of primitive
or other composite messages using a message composing function. In
our logic, we use $\{M_1, M_2, \ldots M_n\}_K$ to represent a message obtained
from encrypting $M_1, M_2, \ldots M_n$ under key K, and use $\{M_1, M_2, \ldots M_n\}$
to represent a message obtained from simply binding $M_1, M_2, \ldots M_n$
together.

We use two specific function symbols in formalizing and reasoning
about cryptographic protocols. Namely, we use $enc(M, K)$ to refer to
the message from encrypting M under key K, and use $dec(M, K)$ to
refer to the message from decrypting M using key K.

Specific Predicates

In order to capture relationships between various objects in cryptographic protocols, we use the following predicates in our logic:

- $send(A, M, B)$ is intended to mean that message M is sent from A to B, where A and B can be either agents or worlds. There are two variants of the predicate: $send(A, M)$ means that a message is sent from A (broadcast); $send(A, M, B_1, B_2, \ldots, B_n)$ means that a message M is sent from A to specific destinations $(B_1, B_2, \ldots, B_n)$.

- $receive(A, M, B)$ is intended to mean that message M is received by A from B, where A and B can be either agents or worlds. It also has two variants: $receive(A, M)$ means that a message is received by A; $receive(A_1, A_2, \ldots, A_n, M, B)$ means that a message M is received by $A_1, A_2, \ldots, A_n$ from B.

- $produce(M, X)$ is intended to mean that object X, such as a key, is produced based on message M, whereas $produce(X)$ simply mean that object X is produced by some agent.

- $shared(X, \alpha_1, \ldots, \alpha_n)$ is intended to mean that X is a shared secret among agents $\alpha_1, \ldots, \alpha_n$. In particular, we mean that K is a shared key between agents $\alpha_1, \ldots, \alpha_n$ by $shared(K, \alpha_1, \ldots, \alpha_n)$.

- $public(K, \alpha)$ is intended to mean that K is a public key of agent α, whereas by $public(K)$ we simply mean that K is a public key.

- $private(K, \alpha)$ is intended to mean that K is a private key of agent α. By $private(K)$ we simply mean that K is a private key.

- $fresh(X, \alpha_1, \alpha_2, \ldots, \alpha_n)$ is intended to mean that as far as agents $\alpha_1, \alpha_2, \ldots, \alpha_n$ are concerned, object X is fresh. We use $fresh(X)$ to simply state that object X is fresh in the current context.

- $commit(\alpha, M)$ means that an agent α commits itself on M. By $commit(\alpha, M, b)$ we mean that an agent α made its commitment on M to agent b.

- $contain(X_0, X_1, X_2, \ldots, X_n)$ is intended to mean that object X_0 contains objects $X_1, X_2, \ldots, X_n$.

- $possess(\alpha, X)$ is intended to mean that an agent α has object X and also knows that it has.

- $trusted(a, b)$ is intended to mean that an agent a is trusted by b. To represent that a is trusted by b on a specific thing, we use $trusted(a, b, \phi)$, where ϕ is some object such as a logical statement.

2.   Axioms and Inference Rules

In this section, we discuss axioms and inference rules of the logic focusing on those that are relevant to cryptographic protocol analysis. We discuss first very briefly some generic axioms and inference rules.

Axiom 1. *(Belief Axioms)*
B1. $\mathcal{B}_\alpha\phi \wedge \mathcal{B}_\alpha(\phi \to \psi) \to \mathcal{B}_\alpha\psi$
B2. $\mathcal{B}_\alpha\phi \to \mathcal{B}_\alpha(\mathcal{B}_\alpha\phi)$
B3. $\neg\mathcal{B}_\alpha\phi \to \mathcal{B}_\alpha(\neg\mathcal{B}_\alpha\phi)$
B4. $\mathcal{B}_\alpha(\phi_1 \wedge \phi_2) \to \mathcal{B}_\alpha\phi_1 \wedge \mathcal{B}_\alpha\phi_2$

The above axioms are from classical belief logic. The attachment of agent labels to modal operator B makes the meaning of the axioms more explicit. For example, Axiom B3 says that if agent α does not believe ϕ is true, then it believes that it does not believe ϕ is true.

Axiom 2. *(Trust Axioms)*
T1. $trusted(a, b) \wedge send(a, \phi, b) \to \mathcal{B}_b\phi$
T2. $trusted(a, b, \phi) \wedge send(a, \phi, b) \to \mathcal{B}_b\phi$
T3. $receive(a, \Phi, b) \wedge trusted(b, a) \to \mathcal{B}_a(\Phi)$

Trust axiom T1 states that if agent b trusts agent a, agent b will believe every fact that has been told by a. Axiom T2 states that if agent b trusts a on a particular thing ϕ and a said ϕ is true, then b will believe ϕ to be true. Trust axiom T3 refers to trust on statements obtained from message passing, and says that if agent a received statement ϕ from b who is trusted by a, then a will believe ϕ to be true.

An agent's beliefs can come from what it has learnt from others. In addition, a logical formula can also become true if it is made true. Thus, we have the following general causal axioms involving the operator "make" $\mathcal{M}$.

Axiom 3. *(Causal Axioms)*
M1. $\mathcal{M}_a\phi \to \phi$
M2. $\mathcal{B}_a\phi \to \mathcal{M}_b\mathcal{B}_a\phi$
M3. $send(a, \phi, b) \wedge \mathcal{B}_b\phi \to \mathcal{M}_a\mathcal{B}_b\phi$
M4. $\mathcal{M}_b\mathcal{B}_a\phi \wedge \mathcal{B}_a(\phi \to \psi) \to \mathcal{M}_b\mathcal{B}_a\psi$
M5. $\mathcal{M}_b\mathcal{B}_a\phi \wedge \mathcal{M}_b\mathcal{B}_a\psi \leftrightarrow \mathcal{M}_b\mathcal{B}_a(\phi \wedge \psi)$
M6. $\mathcal{M}_b(\mathcal{M}_c\mathcal{B}_a\phi) \to \mathcal{M}_b\mathcal{B}_a\phi$
M7. $receive(a, X, b) \to \mathcal{M}_b possess(a, X)$

The first causal axiom M1 says that if agent a has made ϕ true, then we can conclude that ϕ is true. For example, in a court, a witness and the prosecutor can make the judge to have a particular evidence.

Consequently we can say that the judge has the evidence and can use it thereafter. In electronic commerce protocols, a trusted third party, such as a billing server, can act as such a witness. Axiom M2 states that if an agent already believes ϕ, then everyone, including itself, can make the agent believe ϕ; Axiom M3 says that if an agent a said to an agent b that ϕ is true, and a believes ϕ is true, then we can say that agent a "made" agent b believe[1] ϕ; Axiom M4 states that if agent a believes that ψ follows from ϕ, and agent b can make a believe ϕ is true, then we can say that agent b can make a believe ψ to be true as well; Axiom M5 states that if an agent b can make a believe ϕ and if it can also make a believe ψ, then this is equivalent to saying that b can make a believe both ϕ and ψ; Axiom M6 says that if agent b can make agent c to make agent a believe ϕ, then we can say that agent b can make agent a believe ϕ; Axiom M7 says that if an agent a received an object X from b, then we can conclude that agent b made a to have object X.

Axiom 4. *(Message Passing Axioms)*
MP1. $send(a, M, b) \leftrightarrow receive(b, M, a)$
MP2. $receive(a, M, b) \rightarrow receive(a, M) \wedge send(b, M)$
MP3. $receive(b, c, M) \leftrightarrow receive(b, M) \wedge receive(c, M)$
MP4. $receive(b, \{M_1, M_2\}) \leftrightarrow receive(b, M_1) \wedge receive(b, M_2)$

The first four axioms capture the semantics of $send()$ and $receive()$ and their relationships. The meanings of these axioms are straightforward. For example, axiom MP3 says that if both b and c receive the message M, then each one receives it.

Axiom 5. *(Possession Axioms)*
O1. $receive(a, M) \rightarrow possess(a, M)$
O2. $possess(a, \{M_1, M_2\}) \leftrightarrow possess(a, M_1) \wedge possess(a, M_2)$
O3. $possess(a, M_1) \wedge possess(a, M_2) \wedge possess(\alpha, cm)$
$\quad \rightarrow possess(\alpha, cm(M_1, M_2))$
O4. $\mathcal{M}_\alpha produce(X) \rightarrow possess(\alpha, X)$
O5. $\mathcal{M}_\alpha produce(h(X)) \rightarrow possess(\alpha, X)$

Axiom O1 says that if an agent has received something, then the agent has it; Axiom O2 states that if an agent has a message M made from binding two messages M_1 and M_2, then the agent has M_1 and M_2 individually; Axiom O3 says that if an agent has two small pieces of messages and a composing function, the agent has the composed message; Axiom O4 states that an agent has every object it produces; Axiom O5 is about one-way hash functions and says that if an agent α produced a hash value $h(X)$ based on X then we can say α must have object X.

Axiom 6. *(Decryption Axioms)*
$Dp+.$ $possess(\alpha, \{M\}_{K+}) \wedge possess(\alpha, K^-) \rightarrow possess(\alpha, M)$
$Dp-.$ $possess(\alpha, \{M\}_{K-}) \rightarrow possess(\alpha, M)$
$Ds.$ $possess(\alpha, \{M\}_K) \wedge possess(\alpha, K) \rightarrow possess(\alpha, M)$

Axiom Dp+ and Dp- are about the ability to decrypt in public key cryptosystems, whereas axiom Ds is about the ability to decrypt in shared key cryptosystems.

Axiom 7. *(Authentication Axioms)*
$A1.$ $receive(a, \{M\}_K) \wedge \mathcal{B}_a possess(b, K) \wedge \mathcal{B}_a(*c : Agent - [a,b])$
   $\neg possess(c, K) \rightarrow \mathcal{B}_a send(b, \{M\}_K, a)$

This axiom states how an agent can authenticate others: as long as an agent a believes that among all other agents, only b has key K under which the message it received is encrypted, then agent a will believe that the message is from b.

Axiom 8. *(Commitment Axioms)*
$C1.$ $possess(a, \{M\}_K) \wedge \mathcal{B}_a(*x : Agent - [c]) \neg possess(x, K)$
   $\rightarrow \mathcal{B}_a commit(c, M)$
$C2.$ $possess(a, \{b, M\}_K) \wedge \mathcal{B}_a(*x : Agent - [c]) \neg possess(x, K)$
   $\rightarrow \mathcal{B}_a commit(c, M, b)$
$C3.$ $commit(a, \{M_1, M_2\}) \rightarrow commit(a, M_1) \wedge commit(a, M_2)$
$C4.$ $receive(a, \{M\}_K) \wedge \mathcal{B}_a possess(b, K) \wedge$
   $\mathcal{B}_a(*x : Agent - [a,b]) \neg possess(x, K) \rightarrow \mathcal{B}_a commit(b, M)$
$C5.$ $\mathcal{M}_b possess(a, \{M\}_K) \wedge \mathcal{B}_a(*x : Agent - [c]) \neg possess(x, K)$
   $\rightarrow \mathcal{M}_b \mathcal{B}_a commit(c, M)$
$C6.$ $\mathcal{M}_d possess(a, \{b, M\}_K) \wedge \mathcal{B}_a(*x : Agent - [c]) \neg possess(x, K)$
   $\rightarrow \mathcal{M}_d \mathcal{B}_a commit(c, M, b)$

Axiom C1 says that if agent a has object $\{M\}_K$ and it believes that only agent c has the key under which M is encrypted, agent a will then believe that agent c has committed itself on M; Axiom C2 states that if agent a has object $\{b, M\}_K$ and it believes that only agent c has the key K under which M is encrypted, agent a will then believe that agent c has committed itself to agent b on M; Axiom C3 says that if an agent commits itself on a group of objects, it commits herself recursively on every individual object that is readable by the agent in the group. Such commitment, however, cannot be applied to objects that are not accessible to the agent. For example, M_2 could be a message encrypted under a key whose corresponding decryption key is unknown to the agent. Thus the agent cannot be claimed to have made the commitment on the components of M_2; Axiom C4 represents a weaker commitment in shared-key cryptosystems, and says that if an agent a receives a signed message, and it believes that only b and itself have the key K, it will then believe that b has committed on M. Such commitment is weaker in the sense that a will not be able to prove b's commitment to a third party because $\{M\}_K$ may be forged by itself as it also has the key.

In axioms C5 and C6, we have added the modal operator $\mathcal{M}$ to axiom C1 and C2 to indicate how the arbiter can get a piece of evidence, and hence determine who is making the arbiter believe something.

Axiom 9. *(Freshness Axioms)*
F1. $fresh(X_1) \wedge contain(X, X_1) \rightarrow fresh(X)$

Axiom F1 says that if object X_1 is fresh and X_1 is part of X, then X is fresh as well.

Axiom 10. *(Shared Secret Axiom)*
SK. $\mathcal{B}_a shared(X, b, c) \rightarrow$
$\qquad \mathcal{B}_a((*x : Agent - [b, c])(\neg trusted(x, b, c) \rightarrow \neg possess(x, X)))$

It simply states that if agent a believes that a secret is shared among some agents, then it ought to believe that there is no one else having the secret except for the agents who shared the secret or their trustees. But it is not necessary for all these designated agents to actually have the secret at a specific time. For example, a session key in transmission is only known to its generator.

Axiom 11. *(Secrecy Axioms)*
SH. $possess(a, \{M\}_K) \wedge \neg possess(a, K) \rightarrow \neg possess(a, M)$
PB. $possess(a, \{M\}_{K+}) \wedge \neg possess(a, K^-) \rightarrow \neg possess(a, M)$

Axiom SH is about secrecy in shared-key cryptosystems, whereas axiom PB is about secrecy in public-key cryptosystems.

Here are some axioms that can be used to capture the e-commerce properties related to the openness of the network such as the Internet.

Axiom 12. *(Openness Axioms)*
OP1. $send(a, M, b) \rightarrow (!x : Agent - [b, c])receive(x, M, a)$
OP2. $possess(a, M) \rightarrow (* x : Agent)send(a, M, x)$
OP3. $public(K) \rightarrow (*x : Agent)possess(x, K)$

The first openness axiom says that if an agent sends a message to another over an open network, it is possible for a third party to receive the message; The second openness axiom states that if an agent has a message, it is free to send the message to anyone on the network; The last openness axiom is about public keys, and it states that anyone can has a public key.

We only use two inference rules in our logic. The first one is the well-known Modus Ponens rule from the classical first order logic [CH73]:

Rule 1. *(Modus Ponens) From ψ and $\psi \to \phi$ infer ϕ.*

The next is the necessitation rule from the classical modal logic [C95]. It says that if ψ is true in the knowledge base of some agent, we can conclude that the agent believes ψ is true.

Rule 2. *(Necessitation) From $\vdash \psi$ infers $\vdash \mathcal{B}\psi$.*

3. Examples of Protocol Analysis

A cryptographic protocol can be considered as a sequence of actions taken by some agents (or principals). Often, passing messages between agents is the only sort of actions explicitly expressed in protocols. Such an action is commonly represented as $A \to B : M_0, M_1, \ldots, M_n$, where A and B are agents whereas $M_0, M_1, \ldots, M_n$ are messages in either clear or cipher text.

In general, to analyze a protocol using our logic, we need first write down a list of $\mathcal{L}^{ec}$ formulae defining the assumptions under which the protocol is designed to run. We denote these initial assumptions as Σ_0. For each step i of the protocol, we can have three sets of logical formulae which represent the actions to be carried out, the conditions under which the actions are to be done and the goals to be achieved immediately after step i of the protocol, and logical consequences that follow from the run of step i of the protocol. We use A_i' (called step formulae), Ω_i and Σ_i to denote these three sets of formulae.

For a protocol P containing n steps of message passing actions denoted as A_1, A_2, A_3, ..., A_n, the relationships between the formulae mentioned above can be illustrated as follows:

$$
\begin{array}{cccc}
\Omega_1 & \Omega_2 & \Omega_3 & \Omega_n \\
\uparrow & \uparrow & \uparrow & \uparrow
\end{array}
$$
$$\Sigma_0 \mapsto A'_1 \Rightarrow \Sigma_1 \mapsto A'_2 \Rightarrow \Sigma_2 \mapsto A'_3 \Rightarrow \Sigma_3 \ldots A'_n \Rightarrow \Sigma_n$$

where $\Rightarrow$ denotes the production of logical consequences, $\mapsto$ means "enable", and "$\to$" means "implication" in the usual manner.

Let Π be the set of axioms and inference rules of our logic; we then refer to $\Pi \cup \Sigma_0 \cup A_1' \cup A_2' \cup \ldots A_n'$ as the logical theory of the protocol, denoted as Σ. Consequently, the analysis of the protocol can be done either directly or indirectly by proving whether formulae in $\Sigma_1, \Sigma_2, \ldots, \Sigma_n$, $\Omega_1, \Omega_2, \ldots, \Omega_n$ and $A_1', A_2', \ldots, A_n'$ are theorems of the logical theory.

Definition 3. *A formula ψ in $\Sigma_i, (i = 1, 2, \ldots, n)$ is a theorem of theory Σ, denoted as $\Sigma \vdash \psi$, if $\psi \in \Sigma_0$, or is a proved theorem in one of*

$\Sigma_1, \Sigma_2, \ldots \Sigma_{i-1}$, *or can be proved from* $\Sigma_0 \cup A'_1 \cup \Sigma_1 \cup A'_2 \cup \Sigma_2 \cup \ldots A'_i \cup$ Σ_{i-1} *using logical axioms and inference rules of* Π; *A formula* ψ *in* $\Omega_i, (i = 1, 2, \ldots, n)$ *is a theorem of theory* Σ, *if* ψ *is a proved theorem of* Σ_i; *A step formula* ϕ *in* $A'_i, (i = 1, 2, \ldots, n)$ *is a theorem of theory* Σ, *if formulae in the premise are all proved theorems of* Σ_{i-1}.

Theorems in the above definition and their proofs in our logic can have several implications for cryptographic protocol analysis. It thus allows our logic to be used to study various aspects of cryptographic protocols [VWZ00]. However, in this chapter, we shall only focus on accountability requirements for some e-commerce protocols.

As discussed earlier in Section 7, to prove the accountability of an agent P for a statement ϕ involves determining whether the agent can obtain sufficient evidence that can be presented to an arbiter who then believes ϕ is true. If we use $OB(P)$ and $OB(A)$ to denote the sets of objects that P and A has respectively and can be used as evidence, and use $BB(A)$ to denote the beliefs of arbiter A, then the process of proving accountability for ϕ can be described as follows: First, we need to determine what objects are in $OB(P)$, what objects are in $OB(A)$, and what beliefs the arbiter A holds to begin with; second, we need to determine what evidence P needs to tell A and how A can derive its new beliefs, which include the statement to be accounted for. Because the arbiter A derives the belief ϕ using the evidence given by agent P, it can be said that agent P has made A believe statement ϕ, that is, $\mathcal{M}_P \mathcal{B}_A \phi$.

3.1. Example 1: The CMU Internet Billing Server Protocol

Our first example is the public-key version of the Internet Billing System (IBS) developed at Carnegie-Mellon University [OT94]. It can be described as follows:

Price agreement:
  1. $E \to S$: $\{price\ request\}_{K_e^-}$
  2. $S \to E$: $\{price\}_{K_s^-}$

service provision:
  3. $E \to S$: $\{\{price\}_{K_s^-}, item@price\}_{K_e^-}$
  4. $S \to Invoice$: $\{\{price\}_{K_s^-}, item@price\}_{K_e^-}$
  5. $S \to E$: $\{service\}_{K_s^-}$
  6. $E \to S$: $\{service\ acknowledgement\}_{K_e^-}$
  7. $S \to Invoice$: $\{\{service\ acknowledgement\}_{K_e^-}\}_{K_s^-}$

Invoice delivery:

8. $E \rightarrow S :$ $\{invoice\ request\}_{K_e^-}$

9. $S \rightarrow B :$ $\{\{invoice\}_{K_b^+}\}_{K_s^-}$

10. $B \rightarrow S :$ $\{\{invoice\}_{K_s^+}\}_{K_b^-}, \{\{invoice\}_{K_e^+}\}_{K_b^-}$

11. $S \rightarrow E :$ $\{\{invoice\}_{K_e^+}\}_{K_b^-}$

The protocol involves three parties: an end user (E), a service provider (S) and a billing server (B). The whole protocol is divided into three sessions: *price agreement, service provision,* and *invoice delivery.* In each part of the protocol, E and S have their own accountability goals. Let A be the arbiter that the parties go to when a dispute occurs. The accountability goals can then be represented in our logic as follows:

Accountability Goals in price agreement:

$$\mathcal{M}_e \mathcal{B}_a commit(S, price) \qquad \text{(G1)}$$

Accountability Goals in service provision:

$$\mathcal{M}_s \mathcal{B}_a commit(E, item@price) \qquad \text{(G2)}$$

$$\mathcal{M}_e \mathcal{B}_a commit(S, service) \qquad \text{(G3)}$$

$$\mathcal{M}_s \mathcal{B}_a commit(E, service\ provided) \qquad \text{(G4)}$$

Accountability Goals in invoice delivery:

$$\mathcal{M}_e \mathcal{B}_a commit(B, Invoice) \qquad \text{(G5)}$$

$$\mathcal{M}_s \mathcal{B}_a commit(B, Invoice) \qquad \text{(G6)}$$

The first accountability goal for the end user is to be able to prove, or make a judge believe, that the service provider has agreed to sell her the service at a specific price "price". Obviously, the service provider also needs a similar accountability goal to prove that the end user has accepted the price. This is reflected by the second goal which states that the service provider should be able to make the arbiter believe that the end user has accepted the price "price" for the service "item"; Goal three says that the end user should be able to make the arbiter believe that the service provider has provided the service, whereas goal four says that the service provider can prove to the arbiter that the end user has obtained the service that has been provided. The last two accountability goals are for invoices, which state that both the end user and the service provider can prove to the arbiter that the billing server has produced the invoice for them. To reason about the accountability using our logic, we prove the following theorem:

Theorem 1. *All of the above accountability goals can be achieved in the public-key based Internet billing service protocol. That is, all formulae G1-6 are theorems of the logical theory of the protocol in our logic.*

Proof. Here we will not describe the full formalization of the protocol and its logical theory, but only discuss those aspects that are necessary for our proof. Let us prove the first accountability goal.

At step 1 of a protocol run, the service provider receives a message from end user E and consequently has the object $\{Price\ request\}_{K_e^-}$ based on our message passing and possession axioms. According to our open axiom OP3 and decryption axiom Dp-, S can also read "Price request" and respond with "price" to the end user. We will assume that there is a function that allows the service provider to produce "price". S is guaranteed to produce object $\{price\}_{K_s^-}$, and send to E at step 2 (by possession axiom O3).

It is a basic assumption or common belief that in a public-key cryptosystem only the owner has a valid private key while the corresponding public key is available for everyone. Thus, after receiving $\{price\}_{K_s^-}$ from S, the end user E will be able to read the price that S has offered. More importantly, as long as E keeps the object $\{price\}_{K_s^-}$, whenever S denies the offered price, E will be able to make the arbiter believe S has made her commitment on the "price" to E by presenting the object $\{price\}_{K_s^-}$ as an evidence. This is because A should already believe that it is only S who has the private key K_S^-, and according to our commitment axiom C1, $\mathcal{B}_a commit(S, price)$ that follows from the evidence object $\{price\}_{K_S^-}$ given to the arbiter by E.

This proof can be explained, based on the general process described before, as follows: At the beginning of the proof (anytime after step 2), $OB(P)$ contains object $\{price\}_{K_s^-}$, whereas $OB(A)$ is empty. Initially,

$$BB(A) = \{private(K_S^-, S), (*x : Agent - [S])\neg possess(K_s^-)\}.$$

After P has given object $\{price\}_{K_s^-}$ to A, we have

$$OB(A) = \{\{price\}_{K_s^-}\}.$$

From this and the existing beliefs of the arbiter, belief $commit(S, price)$ can be derived using our commitment axioms, and added to $BB(A)$. This can be interpreted as

$$\mathcal{B}_a commit(S, price)$$

Further, we have $\mathcal{M}_p \mathcal{B}_a commit(S, price)$ is true according to axiom M2.

Similarly, we can prove that the other accountability goals can also be achieved in this protocol, because it assures that each agent can have some essential objects signed by the relevant agent after specific steps in the protocol run. Let us consider, for instance, some time after step 6 of the protocol. The end user denies that she has obtained the service provided by the service provider S. As S has at least object $\{service\ acknowledgement\}_{K_e^-}$ in the object base $OB(S)$, she would be able to show this object as evidence to the arbiter (unless she has destroyed the object). Based on basic beliefs in private keys and our commitment axioms, the arbiter would believe that it is the end user E who has signed the "service acknowledgement", and has committed to it.

Note that a critical assumption for achieving any of the above accountability goals is the validity of the keys. This protocol itself doesn't provide any of the parties involved with any means, such as a certificate, for checking whether a key is valid or not. $\Diamond$

3.2. Example 2: Permission Based Payment Protocol

Permission based payment protocol (PBP for short) was proposed in [VM96] and is aimed at overcoming some weaknesses in iKP protocols [IBM]. The protocol involves three parties: a merchant M, a client C and a trusted financial institution F. It can be described as follows:

1. $M \rightarrow C$: $M, Cert_F, Offer, \{h(Offer)\}_{K_M^-}$.
2. $C \rightarrow M$: $C, Order, \{h(Order)\}_{R_C^-}$,
   $\{C, F, m, R_C, TransNo, \{\{h(m, R_C, TransNo),$
   $RequestSlip\}_{psk}\}_{R_C^-}\}_{K_F}$.
3. $M \rightarrow F$: $M, Cert_M, \{F, \{C, F, m, R_C, TransNo,$
   $\{\{h(m, R_C, TransNo), RequestSlip\}_{psk}\}_{R_C^-}\}_{K_F},$
   $h(Order)\}_{K_M^-}$.
4. $F \rightarrow M$: $F, \{F, M, C, yes/no, R_C, m, h(Order), TransNo, T_F\}_{K_F^-}$,
   $\{F, M, C, TransNo, T_F, \{Dkey\}_{K_M}\}_{K_F}$.
5. $M \rightarrow C$: $M, \{Service\}_{Dkey}, \{M, C, TransNo, T_M, h(Service), h(Order)\}_{K_M^-}$,
   $\{F, M, C, yes/no, R_C, m, h(Order), TransNo, T_F\}_{K_F^-}$.
6. $C \rightarrow M$: $C, \{PaymentSlip, h(Servvice)\}_{R_C^-}$.
7. $M \rightarrow C$: $M, \{\{M, C, Dkey, TransNo, T_M', h(Order)\}_{K_M^-}\}_{R_C}$.
8. $M \rightarrow F$: $M, \{M, F, T_M'', \{\{PaymentSlip, h(Service)\}_{R_C^-}\}_{K_M^-}$.
9. $F \rightarrow M$: $F, \{F, M, C, PaymentCompleted, F_F', h(Order), h(Service)\}_{K_F^-}$.

We will not explain in detail the protocol here, but only focus on the accountability goals and use our logic to prove whether these goals can be achieved by the protocol.

Accountability Goal for the Client

For the client, an important accountability goal is to gain the ability to make an authority, such as a Financial Institution F or a judge, believe that the merchant has given the offer. This goal can be achieved after the first step of the protocol. The proof is simple. According to our message passing and possession axioms, after step 1, the client has objects $Cert_M$, $Offer$ and $\{h(Offer)\}_{K_M^-}$, and she can verify the validity of K_M^- using $Cert_M$. She is also able to check whether the $Offer$ in plain text is identical to the one in the hash by decrypting $\{h(Offer)\}_{K_M^-}$ using M's public key that everyone can have using our openness axiom OP3. Consequently, the client will believe that the object $\{h(Offer)\}_{K_M^-}$ is really signed by M, so she believes that M has committed on $Offer$. Note that it is very important for the client C to check whether these two $Offers$ are identical before going any further in the protocol.

According to our causal axioms, whenever the merchant wants to deny the $Offer$, as long as C keeps objects $Cert_M$, $Offer$ and $\{h(Offer)\}_{K_M^-}$, she can present these objects to an arbiter A. In a similar way, the arbiter should be able to derive the belief that M has signed object $\{h(Offer)\}_{K_M^-}$. Based on our commitment axioms, this can be translated into formula $\mathcal{M}_C\mathcal{B}_A commit(M, h(Offer))$. Furthermore, to derive $\mathcal{M}_C\mathcal{B}_A commit(M, Offer)$, A only needs to do the same verification as the client C did.

Accountability Goal for the Merchant

For the merchant M, her prime accountability goal is to be able to make an authority believe that the client has accepted the offer, and accordingly has made the order and agreed to pay for the service. We shall prove that the protocol can still give the merchant the accountability, although it uses only pseudo public key pair psk/ppk in conjunction with a random number R_C.

Firstly, in step 2 the merchant can get objects $Order$, $\{h(Order)\}_{R_C^-}$ and another object which can be read only by F because it is encrypted under F's public key. At this time the merchant cannot see $h(Order)$ yet, because she does not have R_C. But she believes only C has R_C^- by assumption. Therefore, right after step 2 the merchant wouldn't be able to verify whether the $Order$ in plaintext is identical to the one in the hash. However, in step 4, the merchant gets the R_C from F, before she delivers the service to the client. As a result, at this time, the merchant has $Order$, $\{h(Order)\}_{R_C^-}$ and R_C. After decrypting $\{h(Order)\}_{R_C^-}$ using R_C, she also has object $h(Order)$; then she can verify the order, and derive her belief[2] on whether or not $\{h(Order)\}_{R_C^-}$ can be used to make an authority believe the client did make the order. These can be formally represented in our logic as:

$$\mathcal{B}_M commit(C, Order) \wedge possess(M, \{h(Order)\}_{R_C^-})$$

When a dispute occurs, M can give $\{h(Order)\}_{R_C^-}$ to the authority.

From $\{h(Order)\}_{R_C^-}$ and even R_C which C could give, the authority cannot verify the Order and further derive her belief. This is because C cannot be trusted in the dispute. So, F has to be asked, as a witness, to present the original R_C to A. Object R_C would be enough if F is trusted by C, otherwise F should keep the whole object $\{\{h(m, R_C, TransNo), RequestSlip\}_{psk}\}_{R_C^-}$.

With the help of F, $commit(C, Order, M)$ will become A's belief according to our commitment and causal axioms, as A should also believe only C has R_C^-. That is, the following formula:

$$\mathcal{M}_M \mathcal{B}_A commit(C, Order, M)$$

holds. Thus the accountability of the merchant M for *Order* can be achieved.

4. Conclusions

We have presented in this chapter a generic belief logic, and demonstrated with two examples how it can be used to analyze accountability requirements for some e-commerce protocols. Different from other logics that have been proposed earlier for this purpose, our logic deals with accountability using two generic modal operators instead of the specific predicate "canprove".

With few extensions, our logic can also be used for analyzing other aspects of protocols in computer security [VWZ00]. In fact, a key objective of the research is the development of a "generic" logic that can be used to study various properties of cryptographic protocols that are widely used in distributed computing systems. In addition, such a logic could also serve as a theoretical base for building a comprehensive protocol analyser for analyzing the individual features of different cryptographic protocols within the context of distributed services and applications. Our next step is to work out a better semantics for the logic based the one we have in [VWZ01], and to further analyze the soundness and computational complexity of the logic. Then we shall begin to build a protocol analyzer based on the logic we have developed.

Notes

1. Agent a may change to not believing ϕ later. Such situation often occurs in a court when defender's proof is also considered.
2. The merchant can stop the protocol if she found any problem with either R_C or the *Order*.

References

[AT91] M. Abadi and M. Tuttle, A semantics for a logic of authentication. In *Proceedings of the Tenth ACM Symposium on Principles of Distributed Computing*, pp.201-216, 1991.

[B90] P. Bieber, A logic of communication in a Hostile Environment. In *Proceedings of the Computer Security Foundation Workshop III*, pp.14-22, IEEE Computer Society Press, June 1990.

[B97] D. Bolignano, Towards the formal verification of electronic commerce protocols, *Proc. of the tenth computer security foundations workshop*, pp133-146, Rockport, IEEE Computer Society Press, 1997.

[BAN89] M. Burrows, M. Abadi, and R. Needham, A logic of authentication. Research Report 39, Digital Systems Research Centre, 1989.

[C95] B. F. Chellas, *Modal Logic—an introduction*, pp.26, Cambridge University Press, 1995.

[CH73] Chin-Liang Chang and Richard Char-Tung Lee, *Symbolic Logic and Mathematical Theorem Proving*, Academic Press, 1973.

[DS81] D.E. Denning and G.M. Sacco. Timestamps in Key distribution protocols. *CACM*, vol. 24, No. 8, pp.533-536, August 1981.

[FV95] R. Fagin, J.Y.Halpern, Y. Moses, M.Y. Vardi, *Reasoning about Knowledge*, pp.76-80, The MIT Press, 1995.

[G90] L. Gong, *Cryptographic Protocols for Distributed Systems*, Ph.D. dissertation, University of Cambridge, April, 1990.

[GNY90] L. Gong, R. Needham, and R. Yahalom, Reasoning about belief in cryptographic protocols. In *Proceedings of the 1990 IEEE Computer Society Symposium on Research in Security and Privacy*, pp.234-248, 1990.

[IBM] IBM Zurich Research, iKP — a family of secure electronic payment protocols.
www.zurich.ibm.com/Technology/Security/extern/ecommerce/

[K95] R. Kailar, Reasoning about accountability in protocols for electronic commerce, in *Proceedings of IEEE Symposium on Security and Privacy*, pp.236-250, IEEE Computer Society Press, 1995.

[KN98] V. Kessler and H. Neumann, A sound logic for analyzing electronic commerce protocols, Fifth European Symposium on Research in Computer Security: ESORICS 98 (Springer LNCS 1485, 1998), pp345-360, Springer 1998.

[OT94] Kevin O'Toole, The Internet Billing Server Transaction Protocol Alternatives, *Technical Report* INI TR 1994-1, Carnegie Mellon University, 1994. ftp.ini.cmu.edu/billing_server/Transaction_Protocol

[RSW96] R. L. Rivest, A. Shamir, and D. A. Wagner, *Time-lock puzzles and timed-release crypto*, Technical Report, MIT Laboratory for Computer Science, 1996.

[S90] P. Syverson, Formal Semantics for Logics of Cryptographic Protocols, *Proceedings of the Computer Security Foundations Workshop III*, Franconia, NH June 1990. IEEE CS Press, Los Alamitos CA, 1990.

[SVO94] P. Syverson and P.C. Van Oorschot, On unifying some cryptographic protocol logics, In *Proceedings of the Computer Security Foundations Workshop VII(CSFW'94)*, (IEEE), pp.14-28, 1994.

[VO93] P.C. Van Oorschot. Extending Cryptographic Logics of Belief to Key Agreement Protocols (Extended Abstract). In *proceedings of the first ACM conference on Computer and Communication Security*, pages 232-234, November 1993.

[VM96] V.Varadharajan and Y.Mu, On the design of secure electronic payment schemes for Internet, in *Proceedings of Twelfth Annual Computer Security Applications Conference*, pp.78-87. IEEE Computer Society Press, 1996.

[VWZ00] V. Varadharajan, H. Wang and Y. Zhang, Towards a generic logic for the analysis of cryptographic protocols, to appear in Proceedings of the 20th International Conference on Distributed Computing Systems, IEEE Computer Society, April 2000.

[VWZ01] V. Varadharajan, H. Wang and Y. Zhang, a generic logic for the analysis of cryptographic protocols, manuscript, 2000.

Chapter 8

PROVISIONAL AUTHORIZATIONS

Sushil Jajodia

Center for Secure Information Systems
George Mason University, Fairfax, VA 22030-4444
jajodia@gmu.edu

Michiharu Kudo

Tokyo Research Laboratory, IBM Japan Ltd.
1623-14, Shimotsuruma, Yamato-shi, 242-8502, Japan
kudo@jp.ibm.com

V.S. Subrahmanian

Institute for Advanced Computer Studies
Institute for Systems Research and Department of Computer Science
University of Maryland, College Park, Maryland 20742
vs@cs.umd.edu

Abstract   Past generations of access control systems, when faced with an access request, have issued a "yes" (resp. "no") answer to the access request resulting in access being granted (resp. denied). In this chapter, we argue that for the world's rapidly proliferating business to business (B2B) applications and auctions, "yes/no" responses are just not enough. We propose the notion of a "provisional authorization" which intuitively says "You may perform the desired access provided you cause condition C to be satisfied." For instance, a user accessing an online brokerage may receive some information if he fills out his name/address, but not otherwise. While a variety of such provisional authorization mechanisms exist on the web, they are all hardcoded on an application by application basis. We show that given (almost) any logic L, we may define a provisional authorization specification language $\mathsf{pASL}_{\mathcal{L}}$. $\mathsf{pASL}_{\mathcal{L}}$ is based on the declarative, polynomially evaluable authorization specification language ASL proposed by Jajodia et al [JSS97]. We define programs in $\mathsf{pASL}_{\mathcal{L}}$, and specify how given any access request, we must find a "weakest" precondition under which the access can be granted (in the worst case, if this weakest precondition is "false" this amounts to a denial). We develop a model theoretic semantics for $\mathsf{pASL}_\mathcal{L}$ and show how it can be applied to online sealed-bid auction servers and online contracting.

1. Introduction

Almost all studies in access control and authorization systems have assumed the following model: *a user makes an access request of a system in some context, and the system either authorizes the access request or denies it.* Models vary in what types of accesses are being considered (e.g. read, write, query, execute a function, etc.), who makes the request (user, member of a group of individuals, etc.), what objects are being accessed (e.g. file, directory, etc.), and what constitutes the context of the request (e.g. role). However, today's rapidly expanding electronic commerce environment makes such models that either authorize or deny a request overly cumbersome and inflexible. Here are some examples of what we call *provisional authorizations* drawn from real life electronic auctions and business to business e-commerce applications. Intuitively, provisional authorizations tell the user that his request will be authorized *provided* he (and/or the system) take certain actions prior to authorization of his request.

1 **Auctions:** Auctions have now been extensively studied in computer science and game theory [FR96, KF98, MM87, Vic61, Mil89]. Computation auction models consist of a set of business rules and security policies such as ending conditions and confidentiality of the bidding information. For example, in a sealed-bid auction, bids submitted by bidders to the auction server must be kept secret until the closing time of the auction. Moreover, any submission after the closing time must be rejected. Our provisional authorization framework deals with these security policies in a consistent manner. It allows us to say that bidders can submit their bid to the auction server, provided the auction system encrypts the bidding data with specific cryptographic key before it stores in the system, and the system timestamps the bid. These security policies guarantee that the confidentiality of the bidding data and the correctness of the submitted time and can be concisely represented by our provisional authorization language.

2 **B2B commerce:** Consider an online contracting example where one company is looking for a contractor who will conduct a new joint project. Such "matchmaking" services have been studied extensively in the literature [AEK+99]. The primary company put

the contract document securely on the server and other contractors may access it from outside. With our provisional authorization framework, it is possible to say that the contractor can fill-in the contractor field, provided the contractor sends a valid digital signature on terms and conditions statements. In addition to this, the security policy would be that no one other than the contractor can read the contract document once it is signed, and that when anonymous read access to this contract document is denied, the system creates an access history and sends notification mail to the system administrator. All these business and security policy related rules can be handled in the provisional authorization framework we propose in this chapter.

We first lay out a *generic provision based authorization architecture* (Section 2) that extends past proposals for access control to support provision-based access control. Then, in Section 3, we expand on the above auction example and B2B application. These two examples are used throughout the chapter to illustrate basic concepts. Then (Section 4), we describe a *class* of logical languages that may be used for provision specifications, together with some example languages. It is important to note that almost any logic (classical, temporal, Horn clause, etc.) or logic fragment may be used for provision specifications. Next, in Section 5, we will show how an arbitrary provision language $\mathcal{L}$ may be syntactically tied to an authorization language such as ASL (proposed in [JSSB97, JSS97]). The resulting language, called pASL$_\mathcal{L}$, varies based on what provision language $\mathcal{L}$ is chosen. Then, in Section 6, we will develop a formal model theoretic semantics for pASL$_\mathcal{L}$ and prove various theoretical results about pASL$_\mathcal{L}$. Next, we explain the relationship between our work and related work, before concluding the chapter.

2. Provision-based Authorization Architecture

Figure 8.1 shows the architecture of our proposed authorization system. The authorization system assumes the existence of an interface (graphical or otherwise) through which a client can connect to the authorization system. The interface invokes authentication and role checking modules that verify if the user is who she claims to be and whether she is allowed to assume the roles she is assuming in the current interaction. The design and implementation of these modules is beyond the scope of this chapter and may use any existing authentication mechanisms (such as Kerberos [KPS95, SNS88]) and role specification/verification methods [BFL96]. Once a client has been authenticated and the current

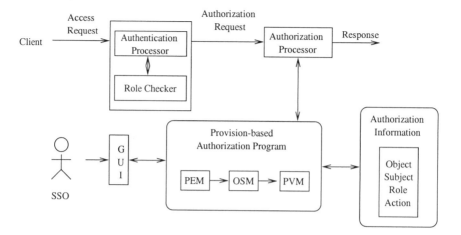

Figure 8.1. Provision-based Authorization Architecture

role verified, the client may make access requests. Each access request involves permission to execute some action a on some object o.

The access request is passed on to a provision evaluation module (PEM) which finds the *weakest* conditions under which the requested access can be honored. For instance, a condition which says the user must fill in her name and address is weaker than a condition which says the user must fill in her name, address and social security number. We will define these concepts formally later. In some cases, the weakest condition may be "true" (resp. false) which effectively means the user is unconditionally authorized (resp. denied) the access. In other cases, the condition may require either the user or the system or both to take certain actions. We will assume that the PEM never asks either the user or system to do impossible things.

Once the PEM finds a weakest condition under which the access may be granted, it passes this condition off to an "Order Specification Module" (OSM for short) which yields a set of ordering constraints on the actions involved. For instance, the ordering constraints may require that the name and address be filled in before the social security number. We will provide a language in which OSM specifications can be written.

Once the PEM finds the weakest conditions under which the access in question may be honored, and the OSM specifies ordering constraints, these conditions are handed off to a *provision verification module* (PVM). This module checks if any of the conditions were previously fulfilled by the client (e.g. if the client had previously provided her name and address) and if so, simplifies the condition (and ordering constraints) and waits till the conditions are satisfied before authorizing the request.

In this chapter, we will focus primarily on the design and implementation of the PEM *and show how our proposed framework is useful in two applications — one relating to electronic auctions and another relating to B2B applications.*

3. Motivating Examples

3.1. Sealed-bid auctions

In an auction of this kind, there are three kinds of participants: Auctioneer, Supplier, and Bidders. First, the Supplier fills in the item to be auctioned, the closing time of the auction, and the minimum price acceptable. Bidders may submit a bid specifying the item and a bidding price if the current time is before the close of the auction and provided the bidding price is encrypted with a timed-release key and the timestamp recording when the bid was received is recorded by the system. Finally, the Auctioneer can fill-in "No good" in the status field if the current time is after closing time and the maximum price of all the bids is lower than the minimum price. or fill in "Completed" in the status field if the maximum price of all the bids is equal or greater than the minimum price.

Figure 8.2 shows (conceptually) the data object and role hierarchies associated with this example. The dotted line in the role hierarchy indicates role assignment to individual users.

3.2. Online Contracting Example

In this scenario, there are two kinds of participants: Requester and Registered Contractor. First, the requester describes a contract *body* and publishes it (e.g. on the Internet). After a registered contractor reads and agrees to the terms and conditions, she or he fills in the name, provided the digital signature on the *contract_body* is written in the contractor signature field with the time of signing the contract and it is verified with the contractor's certificate. Figure 8.3 shows (conceptually) the data object and role hierarchies associated with this example.

3.3. Actions

We summarize actions, provisional actions (to be defined), and external predicates (to be defined) used in the above two examples. There are three actions: read, write, and delete, specified as a single character, r, w, and d, respectively. In some cases, we will have actions $w(v)$ de-

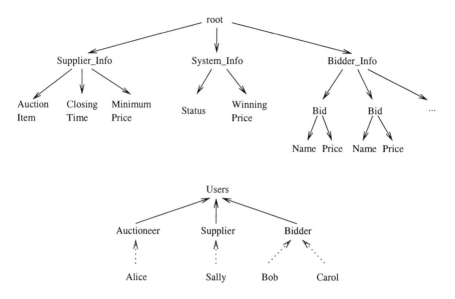

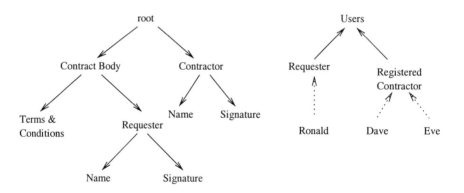

Figure 8.2. Data Object and Role Hierarchies for the Auction Example

Figure 8.3. Data Object and Role Hierarchies for the Online Contracting Example

noting that value v is being written. There are nine provisional actions: encrypt, timestamp, write, get_signed, verify, log, email, reserve_stack, and assignall. These are not limited to the actions listed here but any actions can be defined as an atom if it matches the definition of provision specification language explained in the later section. There are seven "external" predicates (to be described in further detail later): owner, uid, time, field, order, stock_status, and current_top. These predicates are used to retrieve data from external sources.

4.   Provision Specification Language

An *abstract logic* $\mathcal{L}$ consists of a pair $(W_{\mathcal{L}}, Cn_{\mathcal{L}})$ where $W_{\mathcal{L}}$ is any nonempty set (whose elements are called *well formed formulas*, wff's for short) and $Cn_{\mathcal{L}}$ is a mapping (called the *consequence mapping*) from the powerset, $2^{W_{\mathcal{L}}}$, of $W_{\mathcal{L}}$ to $2^{W_{\mathcal{L}}}$ satisfying the following conditions:

- *Inflation.* $X \subseteq Cn_{\mathcal{L}}(X)$.

- *Monotonicity.* $X \subseteq Y \to Cn_{\mathcal{L}}(X) \subseteq Cn_{\mathcal{L}}(Y)$.

- *Idempotence.* $Cn_{\mathcal{L}}(Cn_{\mathcal{L}}(X)) = Cn_{\mathcal{L}}(X)$.

The first axiom says that everything in X must be a consequence of X. The second axiom says that when X is increased by adding new elements to X, this results in potentially new consequences, but all the old consequences remain. The third axiom says that the set of consequences of X is itself closed under the consequence mapping, i.e. applying the consequence operation $n > 1$ times to X is no different than applying it once.

It is easy to see that the above definition of an abstract logic has as a special case, most logics (and fragments of logics) that are in existence today. Below, we show how classical datalog (DL), and (bounded) propositional temporal logic (PTL) may be viewed as abstract logics.

Example 4.1 (Datalog as an abstract logic). *Consider a first order logical language generated by a finite set of constant symbols, predicate symbols and variable symbols. As usual, constants and variables are* DL-terms *and an atom is an expression of the form* $p(t_1, \ldots, t_n)$ *where* $t_1, \ldots, t_n$ *are DL-terms. Wffs of DL are inductively defined as: (i) every atom is a wff, (ii) if F is a wff, then $\neg F$ is a wff, (iii) if F, G are wffs, then $(F \wedge G)$ and $(F \vee G)$ are wffs, (iv) if F is a wff and x is a variable, then $(\forall x)F$ and $(\exists x)F$ are wffs. Consequences of a set X of DL wffs may be defined using standard first order logic model theory [Sho67].*

Example 4.2 (Bounded PTL as an abstract logic). *Propositional temporal logic (PTL) based on an alphabet Σ of propositional symbols has the following inductively defined set of wffs: (i) each member of Σ is a wff; (ii) if F is a wff, then $\neg F, \Box F, \bigcirc F$ are wffs, (iii) if F, G are wffs, then $(F \wedge G)$ and $(F \vee G)$ are wffs. Here $\Box F$ is read as "always F" while $\bigcirc F$ holds at time i if F holds at time $i + 1$. (PTL typically has another derived operator $\Diamond F = \neg \Box \neg F$ read as "eventually F." Suppose time is bounded by an arbitrary but fixed integer N. A temporal interpretation τ associates a set of ground atoms with each $0 \le i \le N$. $\tau, i \models a$ for $a \in \Sigma$ iff $a \in \tau(i)$. $\tau, i \models F \wedge G$ iff $\tau, i \models F$ and $\tau, i \models G$. $\tau, i \models F \vee G$*

iff $\tau, i \models F$ *or* $\tau, i \models G$. $\tau, i \models \neg F$ *iff it is not the case that* $\tau, i \models F$. $\tau, i \models \Box F$ *iff for all* $j \geq i$, $\tau, j \models F$. $\tau, i \models \bigcirc F$ *iff* $\tau, i + 1 \models F$.

$\phi \in Cn_{\mathcal{L}}(X)$ *iff for every* τ, i *such that* $\tau, i \models \psi$ *for all* $\psi \in X$, *it is the case that* $\tau, i \models \phi$.

Definition 4.1 (Implication). *Suppose* $\mathcal{L}$ *is an abstract logic and* ϕ, ψ *are wffs.* ϕ *implies* ψ *if* $\psi \in Cn_{\mathcal{L}}(\phi)$. ϕ *and* ψ *are* logically equivalent *iff* ϕ *implies* ψ *and* ψ *implies* ϕ *and* $Cn_{\mathcal{L}}(\phi) = Cn_{\mathcal{L}}(\psi)$.

It is easy to see that the relation of logical equivalence on wffs of any logic $\mathcal{L}$ is an equivalence relation (i.e., $\mathcal{L}$ is reflexive, symmetric and transitive).

Definition 4.2 (Finitary Abstract Logic). *An abstract logic* $\mathcal{L}$ *is finitary iff the set of equivalence classes of* $W_{\mathcal{L}}$ *is finite.*

Most existing logics generated by finite alphabets are finitary even if they have an infinite set of associated wffs.

Proposition 4.3. *Datalog and bounded PTL as presented in examples 4.1 and 4.2 respectively are finitary.*

Proof.   We prove the result for Datalog. Let k be the maximal arity of any predicate symbol, and let ℓ be the number of constants in our selected datalog language, and n be the total number of predicates in our datalog language. There are at most $(k \times \ell \times m)$ ground atoms in our language. Interpretations (cf. [Sho67]) in propositional logic are sets of ground atomic action terms. Hence there are at most $2^{(k \times \ell \times m)}$ interpretations. Every formula has a uniquely associated set of interpretations, viz. those that satisfy it. Hence $2^{(k \times \ell \times m)}$ is an upper bound on the number of equivalence classes, and so Datalog is finitary.

A similar argument may be made for bounded PTL. Here, all occurrences of $k \times \ell \times m$ above need to be replaced by $N \times k \times \ell \times m$ to obtain corresponding bounds.   ∎

Another important property for an abstract logic to have is that of being *lattice-compliant* which we define below. Given an abstract logic $\mathcal{L}$ and two wffs ϕ, ψ, we say that $[\phi] \leq [\psi]$ iff ϕ implies ψ. In addition, we add two extra elements $\bot$ and $\top$ to $\mathcal{L}$ which are explicit "bottom" and "top" elements of this ordering, i.e. $(\forall x \in \mathcal{L})\bot \leq x \leq \top$. Here, as usual, $[\phi]$ denotes the equivalence class of ϕ. It is easy to see that $\leq$ is a partial ordering on equivalence classes.

Note 1. Throughout this chapter, we assume that our versions of Datalog and bounded PTL are augmented with extra $\bot$ and $\top$ elements as defined above.

Definition 4.4. $\mathcal{L}$ *is said to be* lattice-compliant *iff* $(\mathcal{L}/\equiv, \leq)$ *is a lattice where* $(\mathcal{L}/\equiv)$ *is the set of all equivalence classes of* $\mathcal{L}$.

Proposition 4.5. *Datalog and bounded PTL as presented in examples 4.1 and 4.2 respectively are lattice-compliant.*

Proof. We prove the result for PTL this time. A similar proof applies to DL. It suffices to show that if X is a finite set of wffs not including $\bot, \top$ then X has a glb and an lub (because adding an extra $\bot, \top$ element to a lattice still preserves the lattice property). If $X = \{[\phi_1], \ldots, [\phi_n]\}$ is a finite set of wffs, then it is easy to see that $[\phi_1 \wedge \cdots \wedge \phi_n]$ is the greatest lower bound of X and $[\phi_1 \vee \cdots \vee \phi_n]$ is X's least upper bound. To see why $[\phi_1 \wedge \cdots \wedge \phi_n]$ is the greatest lower bound, note that it is a lower bound as it implies each of $\phi_1, \ldots, \phi_n$. If $[\ell]$ is another lower bound, then ℓ must imply each of $\phi_1, \ldots, \phi_n$, when ℓ must imply $\phi_1 \wedge \cdots \wedge \phi_n$ whence $[\ell] \leq [\phi_1 \wedge \cdots \wedge \phi_n]$. A symmetric argument may be used to establish that $[\phi_1 \vee \cdots \vee \phi_n]$ is X's least upper bound. ∎

Definition 4.6 (Provision Specification Language). *If $\mathcal{L}$ is a finitary, lattice-compliant abstract logic, then $W_{\mathcal{L}}$ is a provision specification language. Nothing else is a provision specification language.*

4.1. Two example provision specification languages

In this section, we provide two example provision specification languages based on fragments of Datalog and temporal logic respectively.

Example 4.3. *Consider a security application involving four finite sets $\mathcal{S}, \mathcal{O}, \mathcal{A}$ of subjects, objects, and actions, respectively, together with sets V_S, V_O, V_A of variables ranging over these respective sets. A subject term is either in S or in V_S. Object terms are similarly defined. Assume that each action has an associated* parameter set *which is finite together with variables over the parameter set. If $a \in \mathcal{A}$, s is a subject term, o is an object term, and z is in a's parameter set or is a parameter variable, then $a(s, o, z)$ is an atom. If a parameter set has an associated ordering on it and t_1, t_2 are parameter terms (constants or variables) then $t_1 = t_2, t_1 \leq t_2, t_1 < t_2, t_1 \geq t_2$ and $t_1 > t_2$ are all atoms. Wffs of this language are obtained by closing the set of such atoms via the connectives $\wedge, \vee, \neg$. In addition, we have the special symbols $\bot, \top$.*

For instance, write(john, namebox, X) is an atom. Likewise read(mary, file1, null) is an atom. In contrast, write(john, namebox, X) $\wedge$ X > 500 is a wff.

Example 4.4. *Consider the sealed bid auction example in Section 3. Here, we have three kinds of atoms:*

1 *encrypt*(*Price*, *Key*) *encrypts a bid amount with a key.*

2 *timestamp*(*Price*, *Time*) *records the time at which a bid was submitted.*

3 *write*(*Field*, *Value*) *writes a specific value into a given field.*

Assuming we know the domain of values from which the arguments of the above parameters are drawn, terms of a given type (e.g. Price, Key, etc.) are either constants from that type's domain or variables ranging over it. If p is a predicate of arity n with arguments having types $(\tau_1, \ldots, \tau_n)$ and $(t_1, \ldots, t_n)$ are terms drawn from these types, then $p(t_1, \ldots, t_n)$ is an atom. Every atom is a wff. In addition, if ϕ, ψ are wffs, then so are $\phi \wedge \psi$, $\phi \vee \psi$ and $\neg \psi$.

Example 4.5. *Consider the online contracting example in Section 3. Here, we have four kinds of atoms:*

1 *get_signed*(*contract_body*, *contractor/signature*) *which has a registered contractor sign on contract_body part and write it into contractor's signature field.*

2 *verify*(*signature*) *which checks if the signature is valid or not.*

3 *log which logs an event;*

4 *email*(*admin*, "*Warning*") *which emails a warning message to the administrator.*

Atoms are defined using the above predicates in the obvious way, and wffs are defined by taking closing the above set of atoms under the operations of conjunction, disjunction and negation.

5. Provisional Authorization Language

In this section, we define an authorization language which extends our previously proposed authorization specification language ASL [JSS97]. Readers familiar with ASL may skip Section 5.1 below.

5.1. Recap of ASL

Given a set of actions A, we define a set of signed authorization types SA as $\{+a, -a \mid a \in A\}$. ASL is a logical language created from the following alphabet:

1 **Constant Symbols:** Every member of $\mathsf{Obj} \cup \mathsf{T} \cup \mathsf{U} \cup \mathsf{G} \cup \mathsf{R} \cup \mathsf{A} \cup \mathsf{SA} \cup \mathsf{IN}$ where Obj is the set of objects, T the set of types, U the set of users, G the set of groups, R the set of roles, A and SA the set of unsigned and signed authorizations respectively, and IN denotes the set of natural numbers.

2 **Variable Symbols:** There are eight sets V_o, V_t, V_u, V_g, V_r, $V_{R,}$, V_a, V_{sa} of variable symbols ranging over the sets Obj, T, U, G, R, 2^R, A, and SA, respectively.

In the following, we refer to elements of a set X and variables ranging over the set as "X terms". For instance, variables in V_o and members of Obj are object terms. We collectively refer to user, role, and group terms as subject terms.

3 **Predicate Symbols:** The following predicate symbols are considered.

   (a) A ternary predicate symbol, `cando`. The first argument of `cando` is an object term, the second is a subject term, and the third is a signed authorization term. The predicate `cando` represents authorizations explicitly inserted by the SSO.

   (b) A ternary predicate symbol, `dercando`, with the same arguments as `cando`. The predicate `dercando` represents authorizations derived by the system using logical rules of inference.

   (c) A ternary predicate symbol, `do`, with the same arguments as `cando`. The predicate *do* represents the authorizations that hold for each subject on each object. It enforces the conflict resolution policy.

   (d) A 5-term predicate symbol, `done`. The first argument is an object term, the second argument is a user term, the third argument is a role-set term, the fourth argument is an unsigned action term, and the fifth argument is a natural number. Done rules represent the accesses executed by requestor subjects.

   (e) A binary predicate `active` whose first argument is a user term and second argument is a role term. It captures the concept of active role/s for a user.

   (f) Two binary predicates `dirin` and `in` that take as arguments two subjects s_1, s_2. They capture the direct and indirect membership relationship between subjects.

(g) A binary predicate `typeof` that takes as arguments, an object o and an object type t. It captures the grouping relationship between objects.

(h) A predicate symbol `error`, with no arguments. If `error()` can be derived through some rule, then there is an error in the specification or use of authorizations due to the satisfaction of the conditions stated in the body of the rule.

If p is one of the above predicate symbols with arity n, and $t_1, \ldots, t_n$ are terms appropriate for p (as defined above), then $p(t_1, \ldots, t_n)$ is an *atom*. We will use the expression *literal* to denote an atom or its negation. For instance, if OT, ST, and SAT are object terms, subject terms, and signed action terms respectively then `cando`(OT, ST, SAT) and $\neg$`cando`(OT, ST, SAT) are examples of literals.

We now define the rules that can be expressed in our language.

Definition 5.1 (Done Rule). *A* done rule *is a rule of the form:*

$$\text{done}(o, s, R, a, t) \leftarrow \ .$$

where o, s, R, a and t are elements of Obj$, \mathsf{U}, 2^R, \mathsf{A}$ *and* $\mathbb{N}$ *respectively. Note that "done" rules are facts, as their body is always empty.*

Done rules are specified only by the system upon execution of accesses. If `done(o, u, R, a, t)` is true, then user `u` with roles in `R` active has executed action `a` on object `o` at time `t`. Done rules are useful for implementing those policies in which future accesses of a user are based on the accesses that the user has exercised in the past (as in the case of the Chinese Wall policy [BN89]).

Definition 5.2 (Authorization Rule). *An* authorization rule *is a rule of the form:*

$$\text{cando}(o, s, <sign> a) \leftarrow L_1 \& \ldots \& L_n.$$

where o, s, and a are elements of Obj$, \mathsf{U} \cup \mathsf{G} \cup \mathsf{R}$, *and* A *respectively, $n \geq 0$, $<sign>$ is either $+$ or $-$ and, for each $0 < i \leq n$, L_i, either a* in *a* dirin*, or* typeof *literal.*

Authorization rules are specified to allow or deny accesses to subjects. The literals in the right hand side of the rules are used to specify conditions that must be verified for the authorization to hold.

The SSO states authorizations through `cando` rules. From the authorizations so specified, further authorizations can be derived by the system through the application of specified derivation rules. To distinguish authorizations explicitly stated by the SSO from the authorizations derived by the system through derivation rules, we use the predicate **dercando** for derived authorizations. Derivation rules are formally defined as follows:

Definition 5.3 (Derivation Rule). *A derivation rule is a rule of the form:*

$$\text{dercando}(o, s, < sign > a) \quad \leftarrow \quad L_1 \& \ldots \& L_n.$$

where o, s, and a are elements of Obj, U ∪ G ∪ R, *and* A *respectively, $< sign >$ is either $+$ or $-$, $n \geq 0$, and $L_1, \ldots, L_n$ are either* cando, dercando, done, in, dirin, *or* typeof *literals. All* dercando-*literals appearing in the body of a derivation rule must be positive.*

Beside being used for expressing propagation of authorizations along subject's hierarchies, due to their generality, derivation rules can also be used to express different kinds of implication relationships between authorizations.

Derivation rules allow the derivation of authorizations on the basis of other authorizations, either derived or explicitly specified by the SSO.

Note that **cando** and **dercando** rules may admit the derivation of both positive and negative authorizations for a given object, subject, and action. The concept of a *resolution rule*, given below, forces a decision to be made. Resolution rules can also be used to force a decision in case **cando** and **dercando** rules do not imply either a positive or a negative authorization for a given object, subject, and action. In such a case the decision is called the *default* decision.

Definition 5.4 (Resolution Rule). *A resolution rule is a rule of the form*

$$\text{do}(o, s, < sign > a) \quad \leftarrow \quad L_1 \& \ldots \& L_n.$$

where o, s, and a are elements of Obj, U ∪ G ∪ R, *and* A *respectively, $< sign >$ is either $+$ or $-$, $n \geq 0$, and $L_1, \ldots, L_n$ are* cando, dercando, in, dirin, done, *or* typeof *literals and every variable that appears in any of the L_i's also appears in the head of this rule.*

A resolution rule states that a subject must be allowed/forbidden to exercise an authorization type on an object.

Note the difference between **do** rules on the one hand and **cando** and **dercando** rules on the other. **cando** and **dercando** rules are authorizations, either positive or negative, specified by the SSO or derived. These authorizations may conflict and, therefore, may not be obeyed by the system. In contrast, do rules state what authorizations the system must consider valid for each authorization subject, on the basis of the existing authorizations, specified or derived.

5.2. Provisional ASL

We assume the existence of a special set of predicate symbols (not in ASL) called *external predicates*, each having an associated arity. As usual, if p is an external predicate of arity n and $t_1, \ldots, t_n$ are terms, then $p(t_1, \ldots, t_n)$ is an *external atom. All external predicates are interpreted over an arbitrary but fixed interpretation Σ as in the case of constraint logic programming [Llo87].*

Definition 5.5 (pASL$_{\mathcal{L}}$ rule/rule set). *Suppose $\mathcal{L}$ is an arbitrary lattice compliant abstract logic, $\mathcal{C}$ is a (possibly empty) conjunction of external predicates, and $Head \leftarrow Body$ is a rule in ASL. If $\phi \in \mathcal{L}$, then*

$$\phi : Head \leftarrow \mathcal{C} \wedge Body$$

is a rule in the language pASL$_{\mathcal{L}}$.

A pASL$_{\mathcal{L}}$ rule-set is a finite set of pASL$_{\mathcal{L}}$ rules.

In future, we will often write $Head \leftarrow Body$ to denote a pASL$_{\mathcal{L}}$ rule because external predicates and ASL predicates are mutually disjoint sets of symbols, and hence we can easily identify the external part of a rule body and the ASL part of a rule body. In such cases, we will often write $Body^{ext}$ and $Body^{asl}$ to denote the conjunction of external (resp. ASL) atoms in $Body$ — of course, either of these conjunctions could be empty.

Intuitively, suppose we consider a pASL$_{\mathcal{L}}$-rule of the form

$$\phi : Head \quad \leftarrow \quad Body.$$

This rule says that if the $Body$ is true, then the $Head$ is true *provided* ϕ is made true.

The following example shows a pASL$_{\mathcal{L}}$ rule-set associated with the Datalog abstract logic.

Example 5.1. *The rule shown below uses Datalog abstract logic for provision specification language.*

$$assignall(Org, Org') : \mathsf{cando}(Org, S, +delete) \leftarrow$$
$$in(S, admin) \wedge dirin(Org, Org').$$

This rule says that if S is in the admin group and Org' is the parent of Org, then S can delete an organization object Org, provided all members *in Org are assigned to the parent organization. This provision is reasonable because members in organization unit being deleted must always belong to some existing organization unit.*

Example 5.2. *The rule shown below uses* ASL *both to express specifications and as the provision specification language:*

$$\mathsf{do}(box1, S, +w) \wedge \mathsf{do}(box2, S, +w) : \mathsf{do}(bid, S, +w(Bid)) \leftarrow$$
$$current\_top(X) \wedge X < Bid.$$

This rule says that a subject S may submit a bid if the submitted bid exceeds the current top bid provided the bidder writes two boxes (e.g. two entries on a form such as name and address).

The following example shows a pASL$_{\mathcal{L}}$ rule-set associated with the bounded PTL abstract logic. When using PTL, we will often use the notation $\bigcirc_i F$ to denote $\underbrace{\bigcirc \cdots \bigcirc}_{i \text{ times}} F$ and $\bigcirc_{\vee i} F$ to denote $F \vee \bigcirc F \cdots \bigcirc_i$ F. Thus, $\bigcirc_i F$ says F will happen exactly i units from now, while $\bigcirc_{\vee i} F$ says F will happen sometime in the next i time units.

Example 5.3. *The rule shown below uses PTL abstract logic for specifying provisions.*

$$\bigcirc_{\vee 5} reserve\_stock(X) : \mathsf{cando}(X, registered\_contractor, +w) \leftarrow$$
$$order(X) \wedge stock\_status(X, ``few").$$

This rule says that a registered_contractor can order an item (entry X) if the stock status is few, provided the reserve_stock predicate returns true sometime in the next five seconds. This rule implements the practical policy that if the requested product is at low inventory levels, then it is necessary to immediately reserve more by connecting to a stock management system — however this should not take more than 5 seconds.

Example 5.4. $(\bigcirc_{\vee 5} reserve\_stock(X) \wedge write(status, ``reserved")) \vee$ $write(status, ``not\_reserved"):$

$$\mathsf{cando}(X, registered\_contractor, +w) \leftarrow$$
$$order(X) \wedge stock\_status(X, ``few").$$

This rule says that a registered_contractor can order an entry X if the stock status is few, provided the reserve_stock predicate returns true in the next five seconds and the status field is written "reserved", or the status field is written "not_reserved".

Given a pASL$_{\mathcal{L}}$ rule set $\mathcal{R}$, the *ASL rule set* associated with $\mathcal{R}$, is obtained by deleting the entries ϕ associated with the rules in $\mathcal{R}$.

The following example shows the ASL rule set associated with the previously shown Datalog and bounded PTL pASL$_{\mathcal{L}}$ rule-sets.

Example 5.5. *The rule shown below is the* ASL *rule set corresponding to the* pASL$_{\mathcal{L}}$*-rule set of Example 5.1.*

$$\text{cando}(Org, S, +d) \leftarrow$$
$$in(S, Admin) \wedge din(Org, Org').$$

This rule says that a subject S can delete an organization object Org, if S is in the Admin group.

Example 5.6. *The rule shown below is the* ASL *rule set corresponding to the* pASL$_{\mathcal{L}}$*-rule set of Example 5.3.*

$$\text{cando}(X, registered\_contractor, +w) \leftarrow$$
$$order(X) \wedge stock\_status(X, ``few").$$

This rule says that a subject registered_contractor can input order entry if the stock status is few.

Definition 5.6 (pASL$_{\mathcal{L}}$ program). *A* pASL$_{\mathcal{L}}$ *rule set is said to be a* pASL$_{\mathcal{L}}$*-program if and only if its associated* ASL *rule set is an authorization program in the sense of [JSS97, JSSB97].*

A pASL$_{\mathcal{L}}$ *program is* positive *if there are no negated atoms in the body of any rule in the* pASL$_{\mathcal{L}}$ *program.*

We now revisit the pASL$_{\mathcal{L}}$ rule-sets associated with the Datalog abstract logic and the bounded PTL abstract logic and show that they are valid pASL$_{\mathcal{L}}$-programs.

5.3. Sealed-bid Auction as a Provisional ASL rule set

r1	cando(supplier_info, X, +rw) ← $in(X, supplier)$.
r2	cando(auctioneer_info,X, +r) ← $in(X, supplier)$
r3	cando(auctioneer_info,X, +r) ← $in(X, bidder)$.
r4	cando(bid, A1, +r)← owner(bid, A1) ∧ uid(A1).

r5	encrypt(Price, key1) ∧ timestamp(Price, tsa1):
	        cando(bidder_info,A1, +w(Price)) ←
	        not(done(bidder_info, A1,+w(Price'))) ∧
	        uid(A1) ∧ time(T) ∧
	        field(closing_time, A2) ∧
	        T <A2.

r6	write(winning_price, -1):
	        cando(status, auctioneer, +w("No Good")) ←
	        current_top(A1) ∧
	        field(minimum_price, A2) ∧
	        A1 <A2 ∧ time(T) ∧
	        field(closing_time, A3) ∧ T >= A3.

r7	write(winning_price, A1):
	        cando(status, auctioneer, +w("Completed"))←
	        current_top(A1) ∧ field(minimum_price, A2) ∧
	        A1 >= A2 ∧ time(T) ∧
	        field(closing_time, A3) ∧ T >= A3.

r8	do(O,S,A) ← cando(O,S,A).

- Rules r1, r2, and r3 say that the supplier can read and write any fields in supplier_info node, and the supplier and the bidder can read any fields in auctioneer section, respectively.

- Rule r4 says that the bidder who submitted bid data can read his/her data.

- Rule r5 says that if the bidder has not submitted a bid before and the current time is before the closing time of auction, the bidder can submit a bid, provided price is encrypted with time release key key1 and timestamp from tsa1 authority is recorded.

- Rule r6 says that if the maximum price of submitted bids is lower than the minimum price and the current time is after the closing time, the auctioneer writes "no good" in the status field in the system_info section, provided error code is written in winning_price field.

- Rule r7 says that if the maximum price of submitted bids is equal or greater than the minimum price and the current time is after the closing time, the auctioneer writes "completed" in the status field in the system_info section, provided the highest price is written in the winning_price field.

- Rule r8 says a subject must be authorized an access if cando(O,S,A) holds.

5.4. Online contracting as a Provisional ASL Rule rule set

r1	cando(*,X, +r)← in(X,requester).
r2	cando(contract_body,X, +w)← in(X,requester) ∧ field(contractor/signature, ").
r3	cando(contract_body,X, +r) ← in(X,registered_contractor).
r4	cando(contractor, registered_contractor, +r)← done(contractor,A1,w,T) ∧ uid(A1).
r5	get_signed(contract_body,contractor/signature) ∧ verify(contractor/signature): cando(contractor/name,X,+w) ← in(X,registered_contractor)) ∧ field(contractor/signature, ").
r6	log ∧ email(admin, "Warning"): cando(*, anonymous, -r).
r7	do(O,S,A) ← cando(O,S,A).

- Rule r1 and r2 says that the requester can read any field in the contract document, and write contract_body if the contractor's signature has not been written yet.

- Rule r3 says that the registered contractor can read contractor_body section.

- Rule r4 says that the registered contractor read any field in the contract_body if s/he wrote the contractor's name field.

- Rule r5 says that the registered contractor can write his name in contractor's name field if the contractor's signature field is not filled, provided his/her signature on contrat_body is written in the contractor/signature field and is verified correctly.

- Rule r6 says that any anonymous read access is not allowed but the access is logged and warning mail is sent to the adiministrator.

- Rule r7 says a subject must be authorized an access if cando(O,S,A) holds.

6. Model Theoretic Semantics

In this section, we provide a model theoretic semantics for pASL$_{\mathcal{L}}$-programs. We define the model theoretic semantics in two steps — first we specify the semantics for *positive* pASL$_{\mathcal{L}}$ programs, and then we extend this semantics to the case of all pASL$_{\mathcal{L}}$-programs.

6.1. Positive P-ASL$_L$ Programs: Model Theoretic Semantics

In this section, we define a formal model theoretic semantics for positive pASL$_{\mathcal{L}}$ programs. As is common in model theory, we will first define the concept of an interpretation. Throughout this section, we will assume that $\mathcal{L}$ is an arbitrary, but fixed abstract logic which is lattice compliant and finitary.

Definition 6.1 ($\mathcal{L}$-interpretation). *An $\mathcal{L}$-interpretation is a mapping from the set of all ground* ASL *atoms to members of $\mathcal{L}$.*

For instance, returning to the two previously shown Datalog and bounded PTL pASL$_{\mathcal{L}}$ rule-sets, the following are $\mathcal{L}$ interpetations.

Example 6.1. *Consider the sealed-bid auction example. An example $\mathcal{L}$ interpretation in this case may be defined as follows:*

Logical Atom	Member of $\mathcal{L}$ assigned to it
$p(supplier\_info, X, +rw)$	$\top$ when X is a supplier and $p \in \{cando, do, dercando\}$.
$p(auctioneer\_info, X, +r)$)	$\top$ when X a supplier or bidder and p is as above.
$p(B, X, +r)$	$\top$ when B is a bid, and X is a bidder and p is as above.
$p(bidder\_info, X, +w(Price))$	$encrypt(Price, zzz) \wedge$ $timestamp(Price, tsa1)$.
$p(status, auctioneer, +w(\text{``No good''}))$	$w(winning\_price, -1)$.
$p(status, auctioneer, +w(\text{``Completed''}))$	$w(winning\_price, 200)$.
all other atoms	$\bot$

It is important to note that only ASL atoms are assigned members of $\mathcal{L}$ by a $\mathcal{L}$-interpretation. External atoms are interpreted according to the interpretation Σ mentioned earlier. It may well be the case (as we have seen above) that $\mathcal{L}$ is a logical language — atoms in the language of $\mathcal{L}$ (if they exist for the selected $\mathcal{L}$) are not assigned members of $\mathcal{L}$ by a $\mathcal{L}$-interpetation !

As we can see from the above definition, $\mathcal{L}$-interpretations assign members of $\mathcal{L}$ only to *ground* ASL *atoms* — we now show how they may be extended to assign members of $\mathcal{L}$ to ASL formulas.

Definition 6.2. *Suppose I is a $\mathcal{L}$-interpretation. Then:*

1 $I(A \& B) = \mathsf{glb}(I(A), I(B))$.

2 $I(A \vee B) = \mathsf{lub}(I(A), I(B))$.

3 $I((\forall X)F[X])) = \mathsf{glb}\{I(F[t]) \mid t \text{ is a constant }\}$.

$4 \ I((\exists X)F[X])) = \mathsf{lub}\{I(F[t]) \mid t \ is \ a \ constant \ \}.$

Here, glb *and* lub *stand for greatest lower bound and least upper bound, respectively, and $F[t]$ denotes the simultaneous replacement of all free occurrences of X in F by t.*

For instance, consider the sample $\mathcal{L}$-interpretation of example 6.1. Here, $\mathsf{do}(bid1, abc, +r)$ is assigned $\top$ and $\mathsf{do}(bidder\_info, abc, +w(50))$ is assigned $encrypt(50, zzz) \wedge timestampl(50, tsa1)$. Thus, $\mathsf{do}(bid1, abc, +r) \wedge \mathsf{do}(bidder\_info, abc, +w(50))$ is assigned the greatest lower bound of $\top$ and $encrypt(50, zzz) \wedge timestamp(50, tsa1)$ which is $encrypt(50, zzz) \wedge timestamp(50, tsa1)$.

Definition 6.3 (satisfying a pASL$_\mathcal{L}$-rule). *An $\mathcal{L}$-interpretation I satisfies the ground pASL$_\mathcal{L}$-rule $\phi : Head \leftarrow Body$ iff either:*

1 There is an external atom in Body such that $\Sigma \not\models Body$ or

2 $\mathsf{lub}(I(Body^{asl}), \phi) \leq I(Head).$

A $\mathcal{L}$-interpretation I is called a model *of a positive pASL$_\mathcal{L}$-rule iff it satisfies every ground instance of it. A $\mathcal{L}$-interpretation I is called a* model *of a positive pASL$_\mathcal{L}$-rule set iff it satisfies every pASL$_\mathcal{L}$-rule in the rule set.*

It is important to note in the above definition that the lattice $\mathcal{L}$ is not applied to the external atoms occurring in a rule — those atoms are interpreted according to the accompanying constraint domain in the standard manner of constraint logic programming [Llo87].

For example, using the sample rules of the Sealed-Bid auction example, it is easy to see that the interpretation of Example 6.1 satisfies rule r4.

Theorem 6.4. *Suppose $\mathcal{L}$ is any finitary, lattice compliant abstract logic and R is any positive pASL$_\mathcal{L}$ rule set. Then R has a model.*

Proof. As $\mathcal{L}$ is lattice compliant, it has a top element $\top$. The $\mathcal{L}$-interpretation I that assigns $\top$ to all ground ASL atoms satisfies R. ∎

Note that when $\mathcal{L}$ is lattice compliant, then we can extend the $\leq$ ordering on $\mathcal{L}$ to an ordering on all $\mathcal{L}$-interpretations as follows: $I_1 \leq I_2$ iff for all ground ASL atoms A, $I_1(A) \leq I_2(A)$. From well known results in lattice theory, it is immediate that the set of $\mathcal{L}$-interpretations is also a lattice under this ordering, and hence, there is a glb and lub operator associated with the set of $\mathcal{L}$-interpretations.

Theorem 6.5. *Suppose $\mathcal{L}$ is any finitary, lattice compliant abstract logic and R is any positive $\mathsf{pASL}_{\mathcal{L}}$ rule set. If I_1, I_2 are models of R, then so is $\mathsf{glb}(I_1, I_2)$.*

Proof. Suppose $\phi : Head \leftarrow Body$ is any ground instance of a rule in R. As both I_1, I_2 satisfy this rule, it follows that either there is a ground atom $A \in Body$ such that $\Sigma \not\models A$ — but in this case, it is easy to see that $\mathsf{glb}(I_1, I_2)$ is immediately a model of the rule, or it is the case that:

$$\mathsf{lub}(I_1(Body^{asl}), \phi) \leq I_1(Head).$$
$$\mathsf{lub}(I_2(Body^{asl}), \phi) \leq I_2(Head).$$

It follows immediately that

$$\mathsf{glb}(\mathsf{lub}(I_1(Body^{asl}), \phi), \mathsf{lub}(I_2(Body^{asl}), \phi)) \leq \mathsf{glb}(I_1, I_2)(Head).$$

But the left hand side of this inequality is the same as

$$\mathsf{lub}(\mathsf{glb}(I_1, I_2)(Body^{asl}), \phi)$$

and hence the result follows. ∎

An immediate corollary of the previous two theorems is that every positive $\mathsf{pASL}_{\mathcal{L}}$ rule set possesses a unique least model.

Corollary 6.6. *Suppose $\mathcal{L}$ is any finitary, lattice compliant abstract logic and R is any positive $\mathsf{pASL}_{\mathcal{L}}$ rule set. Then R has a unique least model which we denote by R^{min}.*

Example 6.2. *Consider the simple example positive $\mathsf{pASL}_{\mathcal{L}}$ program:*

$$\phi_1 : \ \mathsf{do}(o, s, +a) \ \leftarrow \ cando(o, s, +a) \wedge \mathsf{do}(o, s, +b).$$
$$\phi_2 : \ \mathsf{do}(o, s, +b) \ \leftarrow \ cando(o, s, +b).$$
$$\phi_3 : cando(o, s, +a) \ \leftarrow \ .$$
$$\phi_4 : cando(o, s, +b) \ \leftarrow \ .$$

Then R^{min} is the $\mathcal{L}$-interpretation defined as follows:

Logical atom	Member of $\mathcal{L}$ assigned
$cando(o, s, +a)$	ϕ_3
$cando(o, s, +b)$	ϕ_4
$\mathsf{do}(o, s, +b)$	$\phi_2 \wedge \phi_4$
$\mathsf{do}(, s, +a)$	$\phi_1 \wedge \phi_2 \wedge \phi_3 \wedge \phi_4$

Example 6.3. *Consider the simple positive $\mathsf{pASL}_{\mathcal{L}}$ program:*

$$\phi : \mathsf{do}(o, s, +a) \ \leftarrow \ \mathsf{do}(o, s, +a).$$

Then R^{min} is the $\mathcal{L}$-interpretation which assigns $\bot$ to $\mathsf{do}(o, s, +a)$. This says (effectively) that $\mathsf{do}(o, s, +a)$ is denied (there is no proviso under which it is approved).

Suppose we now add the rule $\top : \mathsf{do}(o, s, +a)$. R^{min} is the $\mathcal{L}$- interpretation which assigns $\top$ to $\mathsf{do}(o, s, +a)$. This says (effectively) that $\mathsf{do}(o, s, +a)$ is unconditionally authorized.

We are now ready to return to provisional authorizations and explain how provisional authorizations are computed when the security policy for a given application is expressed via a positive $\mathsf{pASL}_{\mathcal{L}}$ program. Suppose a subject s in role r wishes to perform access a on an object o. This corresponds to an ASL atom $\mathsf{do}(o, s, a)$.

Our security system now tries to compute $R^{min}(\mathsf{do}(o, s, a))$. This is a value drawn from the abstract logic $\mathcal{L}$ in which our provisions are expressed (e.g. a datalog formula or a bounded PTL formula following our previous examples). This constitutes the weakest condition that must be satisfied before the user attempts to execute the desired operation. It is important to note that such a "weakest" condition could be disjunctive and thus reflect a set of possibilities, one of which must be performed in order to satisfy the desired proviso.

Let us reconsider the simple example $\mathsf{pASL}_{\mathcal{L}}$ program of Example 6.2. The simplest precondition to be satisfied for subject s to execute action a on object o is $\phi_1 \wedge \phi_2 \wedge \phi_3 \wedge \phi_4$. In other words, $\phi_1, \ldots, \phi_4$ are four provisions that must all be satisfied for the desired access to be granted.

Example 6.4. *Suppose we now expand the* $\mathsf{pASL}_{\mathcal{L}}$ *program of Example 6.2 by adding one more rule:*

$$\phi_5 : cando(o, s, +a).$$

Then $R^{\min}$ will be:

Logical atom	Member of assigned
$cando(o, s, +a)$	$\phi_3 \vee \phi_5$
$cando(o, s, +b)$	ϕ_4
$\mathsf{do}(o, s, +b)$	$\phi_2 \wedge \phi_4$
$\mathsf{do}(o, s, +a)$	$\phi_1 \wedge \phi_2 \wedge (\phi_3 \vee \phi_5) \wedge \phi_4$

Thus, to satisfy the provisions to be granted access a on object o, subject s must do all of ϕ_1, ϕ_2, ϕ_4, and either ϕ_3 or ϕ_5.

6.2. Arbitrary Provisional ASL Programs: Model Theoretic Semantics

In this section, we show how the model theoretic semantics for positive $\mathsf{pASL}_{\mathcal{L}}$ programs may be extended to the case of arbitrary $\mathsf{pASL}_{\mathcal{L}}$ programs. Recall that the ASL program associated with any $\mathsf{pASL}_{\mathcal{L}}$ program is a locally stratified logic program [Prz88]. This is because the set of predicate symbols occurring in an ASL program is:

Predicate	Rules defining predicate
`hie`-predicates	base relations.
`rel`-predicates	base relations.
`done`	base relation.
`cando`	body may contain `done`, `hie`- and `rel`-literals.
`dercando`	body may contain `cando`, `dercando`, `done`, `hie`-, and `rel`- literals. Occurrences of `dercando` literals must be positive.
`do`	in the case when head is of the form `do(_, _, +a)` body may contain `cando`, `dercando`, `done`, `hie`- and `rel`- literals.
`do`	in the case when head is of the form `do(_, _, -a)` body contains just one literal $\neg(\text{do}(o, u, +a)$.

We may split any $\mathsf{pASL}_\mathcal{L}$ program R into layers as follows.

- Layer R_1: Put all rules having atoms `cando`$(\_, \_, \_)$ in rule heads into layer R_1.

- Layer R_2: Put all rules having atoms `dercando`$(\_, \_, \_)$ in rule heads into layer R_2.

- Layer R_3: Put all rules having atoms `do`$(-, -, +a)$ in rule heads into layer R_3.

- Layer R_4: Put all rules having atoms `do`$(-, -, -a)$ n rule heads into layer R_4.

In the ASL framework, `hie`-predicates, `rel`-predicates, and `done` are all extensional predicate (base predicates) that are not represented via rules. They have the same "status" as the so-called external predicates/atoms that we introduced earlier.

We may now define the semantics of a $\mathsf{pASL}_\mathcal{L}$ program $R = R_1 \cup \ldots \cup R_4$ as follows. As R_1 is a positive $\mathsf{pASL}_\mathcal{L}$ program, its semantics is model theoretically obtained as R_1^{min} as described in the preceding section. Hence, in this section, we specify how to obtain the semantics, R_{i+1}^{min} of R_{i+1} from the semantics of R_i^{min} for $i \leq 3$.

Before doing so, we specify the notion of a *complemented lattice*. Whenever $\mathcal{L}$ is a lattice, a *complement operator* on $\mathcal{L}$ is a mapping, $\mathsf{compl} : \mathcal{L} \to \mathcal{L}$ such that:

$$(\forall x \in \mathcal{L})\mathsf{glb}(x, \mathsf{compl}(x)) = \perp \wedge \mathsf{lub}(x, \mathsf{compl}(x)) = \top.$$

It is easy to see — in our abstract Datalog and PTL examples — that the complement of a formula ϕ is $\neg\phi$. A lattice is said to be *complemented* iff it has an associated complement operator. In the rest of this chapter, we will assume that $\mathcal{L}$ is a complemented lattice.

Definition 6.7. *Consider a $\mathsf{pASL}_{\mathcal{L}}$ program split into layers, and suppose R_{i+1}, $i \geq 1$, is one of these layers. Suppose the semantics $R_1^{min}, \ldots$, R_j^{min} of $R_1, \ldots, R_j$ where $j \leq 1$ are known. Then an $\mathcal{L}$ interpretation I for the atoms in R_{i+1} satisfies a ground instance*

$$\phi : \ Head \ \leftarrow \ Body$$

if and only if either there is a ground atom A in $Body^{ext}$ such that $\Sigma \not\models A$ or $\mathsf{lub}(I(Body^{asl}), \phi) \leq I(Head)$ where $I(Body^{asl})$ is $\mathsf{glb}(\{R_j^{min}(Body_j^{asl}) \mid j \leq i\} \cup \{I(Body_{i+1}^{asl})\}$ where $Body_j^{asl}$ denotes the conjunction of literals in $Body^{asl}$ whose heads occur in rules of layer j and $R_j^{min}(\neg A) = \mathsf{compl}(R_j^{min}(A))$. We now define $R_{i+1}^{min}(Head) = \mathsf{glb}\{I(Head) \mid I \text{ satisfies all rules in } R_{i+1}\}$.

When a user u wishes to make an access a on an object o, all that is needed is to compute $R_5^{min}(\mathsf{do}(o, s, +a))$ — if these precondition is satisfied (e.g. by the user taking some actions, or by the system taking some actions, then the authorization is granted). Otherwise it is not.

Let us consider the following simple example.

Example 6.5. *Suppose we expand the rule set of Example 6.2 via the addition of the rule:*

$$\phi_6 : \mathsf{do}(o, s, +c) \ \leftarrow \ \neg \mathsf{do}(o, s, +a).$$

Then the semantics of this $\mathsf{pASL}_{\mathcal{L}}$ program is identical to that of Example 6.2 except that $\mathsf{do}(o, s, +c)$ is assigned

$$\neg(\phi_1 \wedge (\phi_3 \vee \phi_5) \wedge \phi_2 \wedge \phi_4).$$

This basically says that user s is allowed to execute c on object o provided either she did not do one of ϕ_1, ϕ_2, ϕ_4 or she did not do both ϕ_3, ϕ_5.

7.   Related Work

Early authorization models have been largely inflexible and hardcoded a single access control policy [Den83, CFMS94]. Recent work by Woo and Lam [WL93] and by Jajodia, Samarati, and Subrahmanian [JSS97, JSSB97] aims at providing a general framework that is able to support multiple access control policies. All these models, however, assume that the system either authorizes the access request or denies it. In this chapter we have chosen to extend the ASL language [JSS97, JSSB97] because it has a well-understood syntax and semantics. Our extensions enable the authorization system to return more flexible access decisions by providing provision verification module, as explained in Section 2.

The concept of provisions bears some similarity to the trigger function supported in several database product (DB2, Oracle, and others). Although the trigger function is capable of specifying necessary set of actions in SQL that must follow some operation, triggers cannot be used in the access control language and to make access control decisions.

PolicyMaker [BFL96] and KeyNote [BFIK] are certificate authorization languages that facilitate policies based on credentials or trust relationship. The access control rules are termed "assertion." An assertion is specified with respect to an issuer, a subject to whom trust is delegated, and a predicate which specifies the class of actions delegated together with the conditions under which the delegations applies. Although they claim that any language can be used as a filter language in PolicyMaker and provides a basic mechanism for supporting partially authorized requests, the filter language is mainly used for specifying conditional expressions and they do not provide theoretic semantics for filter language in PolicyMaker. In KeyNote, provisions have a Condition field that basically consists of a Test field and a Value field, the former indicates conditional expressions and the latter the value that is returned to the application (such as No_Access/Limited_Access/Full_Access and ApproveAndLog/ RejectButLog). Although the applications can define any values as they want, authors provide no explicit semantics for them. We deal with application specific authorizations as follows: First we separate the application specific notion from the primitive access control notion. Next we provide theoretical semantics for combining these two notions. In other words, provision specification language corresponds to application specific actions defined by each applications, and the original ASL language to the basic authorization specification mechanism.

There are several application models for auctions. Franklin and Reiter modeled sealed-bid auction by using cryptographic technique in order to avoid single point of trust [FR96]. Thus they need several special-purpose auction servers and specific cryptographic programs. On the other hand, we are focusing on the expressiveness for specifying access control policy that enables the policy programmer to specify sealed-bid auction very easily. The sealed-bid auction is differently modeled by introducing time-release cryptography in [Kud98]. The auction example used in the previous sections borrows the idea of time-key that protects time-sensitive confidential data such as sealed-bid and combines that notion in the provisional expression as a generic encryption operation.

8. Conclusions

Access control models typically assume that the system issues "yes/no" decisions either authorizing or denying an access request. However, there is a growing number of B2B applications that require that "yes/no" decisions be replaced by "yes if some actions are taken by the user or the system, no otherwise." In this chapter, we developed pASL$_\mathcal{L}$, an extension of our previous authorization language ASL [JSS97, JSSB97], to provide conditional authorizations. This extension required not only reworking of the syntax of the authorization specification language but its sematics as well.

Currently, we are implementing the various components of the provision based authorization architecture shown in Figure 8.1. Our goal is to demonstrate the feasilty of our approach by using our system in a wide variety of diverse B2B applications.

References

[AEK$^+$99] K. Arisha, T. Eiter, S. Kraus, F. Ozcan, R. Ross, and V. S. Subrahmanian. IMPACT: Interactive Maryland Platform for Agents Collaborating Together. *IEEE Intelligent Systems*, pages 64–72, March 1999.

[BFIK] M. Blaze, J. Feigenbaum, J. Ioannidis, and A. Keromytis. The KeyNote trust management system (version 2). Technical report, Internet RFC, http://www.cis.upenn.edu/angelos/Papers/rfcnnnn.txt.

[BFL96] M. Blaze, J. Feigenbaum, and J. Lacy. Decentralized trust management. In *Proc. IEEE Symp. on Security and Privacy*, pages 164–173, May 1996.

[BN89] D. F. C. Brewer and M. J. Nash. The Chinese wall security policy. In *Proc. Symp. on Security and Privacy*, pages 215–228, Oakland, CA, May 1989.

[CFMS94] Silvana Castano, Mariagrazia Fugini, Giancarlo Martella, and Pierangela Samarati. *Database Security*. Addison-Wesley, Reading, MA, 1994.

[Den83] Dorothy E. Denning. *Cryptography and Data Security*. Addison-Wesley, Reading, MA, 1983.

[FR96] M. K. Franklin and M. K. Reiter. The design and implementation of a secure auction service. *IEEE Trans. on Software Engineering*, 22(5):302–312, May 1996.

[JSS97] Sushil Jajodia, Pierangela Samarati, and V. S. Subrahmanian. A logical language for expressing authorizations. In *Proc. IEEE Symp. on Security and Privacy*, pages 31–42, Oakland, CA, May 1997.

[JSSB97] Sushil Jajodia, Pierangela Samarati, V. S. Subrahmanian, and Elisa Bertino. A unified framework for enforcing multiple access control policies. In *Proc. ACM SIGMOD Int'l. Conf. on Management of Data*, pages 474–485, Tucson, AZ, May 1997.

[KF98] Manoj Kumar and Stuart I. Feldman. Internet auctions. In *Third USENIX Workshop on Electronic Commerce*, 1998.

[KPS95] Charlie Kaufman, Radia Perlman, and Make Speciner. *Network Security: Private Communication in a Public World*. Prentice–Hall, Englewood Cliffs, NJ, 1995.

[Kud98] Michiharu Kudo. Secure electronic sealed-bid auction protocol with public key cryptography. *IEICE Transactions on Fundamentals of Electronics, Communications and Computer Sciences*, E81-A(1), January 1998.

[Llo87] J. W. Lloyd. *Foundations of Logic Programming*. Springer, 1987.

[Mil89] Paul Milgrom. Auctions and bidding: A primer. *Journal of Economic Perspectives*, 3(3):3–22, Summer 1989.

[MM87] R.P McAfee and John McMillan. Auctions and bidding. *Journal of Economic Literature*, 25(2):699–738, June 1987.

[Prz88] T. Przymusinski. On the declarative semantics of deductive databases and logic programs. In J. Minker, editor, *Foundations of deductive databases*, pages 193–216. Morgan Kaufmann, San Mateo, 1988.

[Sho67] J. Shoenfield. *Mathematical Logic*. Addison Wesly, 1967.

[SNS88] J. G. Stener, B. C. Neuman, and J. I. Schiller. Kerberos: An authentication service for open network systems. In *Proc. USENIX Conf.*, February 1988.

[Vic61] David Vickrey. Counter speculation, auctions, and competitive sealed tenders. *Journal of Finance*, pages 9–37, March 1961.

[WL93] Thomas Y. C. Woo and Simon S. Lam. Authorizations in distributed systems: A new approach. *Journal of Computer Security*, 2(2,3):107–136, 1993.

Index